Your Office

Getting Started with Project Management Using Microsoft® Project 2013

Amy Kinser

KRISTYN A. JACOBSON

PEARSON

Boston Columbus Indianapolis New York San Francisco Upper Saddle River
Amsterdam Cape Town Dubai London Madrid Milan Munich Paris Montréal Toronto
Delhi Mexico City São Paulo Sydney Hong Kong Seoul Singapore Taipei Tokyo

VP of Career Skills: Andrew Gilfillan
Senior Editor: Samantha McAfee Lewis
Team Lead, Project Management: Laura Burgess
Project Manager: Anne Garcia
Program Manager: Natacha Moore
Development Editor: Vonda Keator, Keator & Pen
Editorial Assistant: Victoria Lasavath
Director of Product Marketing: Maggie Waples
Director of Field Marketing: Leigh Ann Sims
Field Marketing Managers: Brad Forrester & Joanna Sabella

Marketing Coordinator: Susan Osterlitz
Senior Operations Specialist: Maura Zaldivar
Senior Art Director: Diane Ernsberger
Interior and Cover Design: Diane Ernsberger
Associate Director of Design: Blair Brown
Digital Media Editor: Eric Hakanson
Director of Media Development: Taylor Ragan
Media Project Manager, Production: John Cassar
Full-Service Project Management: GEX Publishing Services
Composition: GEX Publishing Services

Credits and acknowledgments borrowed from other sources and reproduced, with permission, in this textbook appear on the appropriate page within text.

Library of Congress Control Number: 2014940715

3 16
ISBN-13: 978-0-13-314399-7
ISBN-10: 0-13-314399-6

About the Authors

Amy S. Kinser, Esq., Series Editor

Amy holds a B.A. degree in Chemistry with a Business minor from Indiana University, and a J.D. from the Maurer School of Law, also at Indiana University. After working as an environmental chemist, starting her own technology consulting company, and practicing intellectual property law, she has spent the past 12 years teaching technology at the Kelley School of Business in Bloomington, Indiana—#1 ranked school for undergraduate program performance in the specialty of Information Systems according to 2012 Bloomberg Businessweek. Currently, she serves as the Director of Computer Skills and Senior Lecturer at the Kelley School of Business at Indiana University. She also loves spending time with her two sons, Aidan and J. Matthew, and her husband J. Eric.

I dedicate this series to my Kinser Boyz for their unwavering love, support, and patience; to my family; to my students for inspiring me; to Sam for believing in me; and to the instructors. I hope this series will inspire!
Amy Kinser

Kristyn A. Jacobson

Kristyn holds an M.S. in Education from the University of Wisconsin-La Crosse and a B.S. in Business Education from the University of Wisconsin-Eau Claire. She has been a faculty member and department chair of the Business Technology Department at Madison College in Madison, Wisconsin, for more than 10 years. As well as teaching, Kristyn provides training to businesses on the Microsoft Office Suite including MS Project, project management, customer service, personal productivity, and time management. Kristyn has also worked with companies to personalize an MS Project plan to fit their specific needs. Prior to teaching at Madison College, she taught at a business college in Des Moines, Iowa. There she helped research, design, and develop their online learning program while also teaching traditional business courses.

I dedicate this book to the three most imaginative, exciting, and encouraging pages in my book of life: Paige, Emma, and Jerra Joe!
Kristyn Jacobson

Contents

Acknowledgments

The *Your Office* team would like to thank the following reviewers who have invested time and energy to help shape this series from the very beginning, providing us with invaluable feedback through their comments, suggestions, and constructive criticism.

We'd like to especially thank our Focus Group attendees and User Diary Reviewers:

Heather Albinger
Waukesha County Technical College

Melody Alexander
Ball State University

Mazhar Anik
Owens Community College

David Antol
Hartford Community College

Cheryl Brown
Delgado Community College

Janet Campbell
Dixie State College

Kuan Chen
Purdue Calumet

Jennifer Day
Sinclair Community College

Joseph F. Domagala
Duquesne University

Christa Fairman
Arizona Western University

Denise Farley
Sussex County Community College

Drew Foster
Miami University of Ohio

Lorie Goodgine
Tennessee Technology Center in Paris

Jane L. Hammer
Valley City State University

Kay Johnson
Community College of Rhode Island

Susumu Kasai
Salt Lake Community College

Linda Kavanaugh
Robert Morris University

Jennifer Krou
Texas State University, San Marcos

Michelle Mallon
Ohio State University

Sandra McCormack
Monroe Community College

Melissa Nemeth
Indiana University – Purdue University, Indianapolis

Janet Olfert
North Dakota State University

Patsy Ann Parker
Southwestern Oklahoma State University

Cheryl Reindl-Johnson
Sinclair Community College

Jennifer Robinson
Trident Technical College

Tony Rose
Miami University of Ohio

Cindi Smatt
North Georgia College & State University

Jenny Lee Svelund
University of Utah

William VanderClock
Bentley University

Jill Weiss
Florida International University

Lin Zhao
Purdue Calumet

We'd like to thank all of our conscientious reviewers, including those who contributed to our previous editions:

Sven Aelterman
Troy University

Nitin Aggarwal
San Jose State University

Angel Alexander
Piedmont Technical College

Melody Alexander
Ball State University

Karen Allen
Community College of Rhode Island

Maureen Allen
Elon University

Wilma Andrews
Virginia Commonwealth University

Mazhar Anik
Owens Community College

David Antol
Harford Community College

Kirk Atkinson
Western Kentucky University

Barbara Baker
Indiana Wesleyan University

Kristi Berg
Minot State University

Kavuri Bharath
Old Dominion University

Ann Blackman
Parkland College

Jeanann Boyce
Montgomery College

Lynn Brooks
Tyler Junior College

Cheryl Brown
Delgado Community College, West Bank Campus

Bonnie Buchanan
Central Ohio Technical College

Peggy Burrus
Red Rocks Community College

Richard Cacace
Pensacola State College

Margo Chaney
Carroll Community College

Shanan Chappell
College of the Albemarle, North Carolina

Kuan Chen
Purdue Calumet

David Childress
Ashland Community and Technical College

Keh-Wen Chuang
Purdue University, North Central

Suzanne Clayton
Drake University

Amy Clubb
Portland Community College

Bruce Collins
Davenport University

Margaret Cooksey
Tallahassee Community College

Charmayne Cullom
University of Northern Colorado

Christy Culver
Marion Technical College

Juliana Cypert
Tarrant County College

Harold Davis
Southeastern Louisiana University

Jeff Davis
Jamestown Community College

Jennifer Day
Sinclair Community College

Anna Degtyareva
Mt. San Antonio College

Beth Deinert
Southeast Community College

Kathleen DeNisco
Erie Community College

Donald Dershem
Mountain View College

Bambi Edwards
Craven Community College

Elaine Emanuel
Mt. San Antonio College

Diane Endres
Ancilla College

Nancy Evans
Indiana University – Purdue University,
Indianapolis

Christa Fairman
Arizona Western College

Marni Ferner
University of North Carolina, Wilmington

Paula Fisher
Central New Mexico Community College

Linda Fried
University of Colorado, Denver

Diana Friedman
Riverside Community College

Susan Fry
Boise State University

Virginia Fullwood
Texas A&M University, Commerce

Janos Fustos
Metropolitan State College of Denver

John Fyfe
University of Illinois at Chicago

Saiid Ganjalizadeh
The Catholic University of America

Randolph Garvin
Tyler Junior College

Diane Glowacki
Tarrant County College

Jerome Gonnella
Northern Kentucky University

Connie Grimes
Morehead State University

Debbie Gross
Ohio State University

Babita Gupta
California State University,
Monterey Bay

Lewis Hall
Riverside City College

Jane Hammer
Valley City State University

Marie Hartlein
Montgomery County Community College

Darren Hayes
Pace University

Paul Hayes
Eastern New Mexico University

Mary Hedberg
Johnson County Community College

Lynda Henrie
LDS Business College

Deedee Herrera
Dodge City Community College

Marilyn Hibbert
Salt Lake Community College

Jan Hime
University of Nebraska, Lincoln

Cheryl Hinds
Norfolk State University

Mary Kay Hinkson
Fox Valley Technical College

Margaret Hohly
Cerritos College

Brian Holbert
Spring Hill College

Susan Holland
Southeast Community College

Anita Hollander
University of Tennessee, Knoxville

Emily Holliday
Campbell University

Stacy Hollins
St. Louis Community College,
Florissant Valley

Mike Horn
State University of New York, Geneseo

Christie Hovey
Lincoln Land Community College

Margaret Hvatum
St. Louis Community College, Meramec

Jean Insinga
Middlesex Community College

Jon (Sean) Jasperson
Texas A&M University

Glen Jenewein
Kaplan University

Gina Jerry
Santa Monica College

Dana Johnson
North Dakota State University

Mary Johnson
Mt. San Antonio College

Linda Johnsonius
Murray State University

Carla Jones
Middle Tennessee State University

Susan Jones
Utah State University

Nenad Jukic
Loyola University, Chicago

Sali Kaceli
Philadelphia Biblical University

Sue Kanda
Baker College of Auburn Hills

Robert Kansa
Macomb Community College

Susumu Kasai
Salt Lake Community College

Linda Kavanaugh
Robert Morris University

Debby Keen
University of Kentucky

Mike Kelly
Community College of Rhode Island

Melody Kiang
California State University, Long Beach

Lori Kielty
College of Central Florida

Richard Kirk
Pensacola State College

Dawn Konicek
Blackhawk Tech

John Kucharczuk
Centennial College

David Largent
Ball State University

Frank Lee
Fairmont State University

Luis Leon
The University of Tennessee at Chattanooga

Freda Leonard
Delgado Community College

Julie Lewis
Baker College, Allen Park

Suhong Li
Bryant University

Renee Lightner
Florida State College

John Lombardi
South University

Rhonda Lucas
Spring Hill College

Adriana Lumpkin
Midland College

Lynne Lyon
Durham College

Nicole Lytle
California State University,
San Bernardino

Donna Madsen
Kirkwood Community College

Susan Maggio
Community College of Baltimore County

Kim Manning
Tallahassee Community College

Paul Martin
Harrisburg Area Community College

Cheryl Martucci
Diablo Valley College

Sebena Masline
Florida State College of Jacksonville

Sherry Massoni
Harford Community College

Lee McClain
Western Washington University

Sandra McCormack
Monroe Community College

Sue McCrory
Missouri State University

Barbara Miller
University of Notre Dame

Michael O. Moorman
Saint Leo University

Kathleen Morris
University of Alabama

Alysse Morton
Westminster College

Elobaid Muna
University of Maryland Eastern Shore

Jackie Myers
Sinclair Community College

Russell Myers
El Paso Community College

Bernie Negrete
Cerritos College

Melissa Nemeth
Indiana University – Purdue University,
Indianapolis

Jennifer Nightingale
Duquesne University

Kathie O'Brien
North Idaho College

Michael Ogawa
University of Hawaii

Rene Pack
Arizona Western College

Patsy Parker
Southwest Oklahoma State University

Laurie Patterson
University of North Carolina, Wilmington

Alicia Pearlman
Baker College

Diane Perreault
Sierra College and California State University,
Sacramento

Theresa Phinney
Texas A&M University

Vickie Pickett
Midland College

Marcia Polanis
Forsyth Technical Community College

Rose Pollard
Southeast Community College

Stephen Pomeroy
Norwich University

Leonard Presby
William Paterson University

Donna Reavis
Delta Career Education

Eris Reddoch
Pensacola State College

James Reddoch
Pensacola State College

Michael Redmond
La Salle University

Terri Rentfro
John A. Logan College

Vicki Robertson
Southwest Tennessee Community College

Dianne Ross
University of Louisiana at Lafayette

Ann Rowlette
Liberty University

Amy Rutledge
Oakland University

Candace Ryder
Colorado State University

Joann Segovia
Winona State University

Eileen Shifflett
James Madison University

Sandeep Shiva
Old Dominion University

Robert Sindt
Johnson County Community College

Cindi Smatt
Texas A&M University

Edward Souza
Hawaii Pacific University

Nora Spencer
Fullerton College

Alicia Stonesifer
La Salle University

Cheryl Sypniewski
Macomb Community College

Arta Szathmary
Bucks County Community College

Nasser Tadayon
Southern Utah University

Asela Thomason
California State University Long Beach

Nicole Thompson
Carteret Community College

Terri Tiedema
Southeast Community College, Nebraska

Lewis Todd
Belhaven University

Barb Tollinger
Sinclair Community College

Allen Truell
Ball State University

Erhan Uskup
Houston Community College

Lucia Vanderpool
Baptist College of Health Sciences

Michelle Vlaich-Lee
Greenville Technical College

Barry Walker
Monroe Community College

Rosalyn Warren
Enterprise State Community College

Sonia Washington
Prince George's Community College

Eric Weinstein
Suffolk County Community College

Jill Weiss
Florida International University

Lorna Wells
Salt Lake Community College

Rosalie Westerberg
Clover Park Technical College

Clemetee Whaley
Southwest Tennessee Community College

Kenneth Whitten
Florida State College of Jacksonville

MaryLou Wilson
Piedmont Technical College

John Windsor
University of North Texas

Kathy Winters
University of Tennessee, Chattanooga

Nancy Woolridge
Fullerton College

Jensen Zhao
Ball State University

Martha Zimmer
University of Evansville

Molly Zimmer
University of Evansville

Mary Anne Zlotow
College of DuPage

Matthew Zullo
Wake Technical Community College

Additionally, we'd like to thank our MyITLab team for their review and collaboration with our text authors:

LeeAnn Bates

Jennifer Hurley

Ralph Moore

Jerri Williams

Jaimie Noy
Media Producer

Preface

The **Your Office** series focuses first and foremost on preparing students to use both technical and soft skills in the real world. Our goal is to provide this to both instructors and students through a modern approach to teaching and learning Microsoft Office applications, an approach that weaves in the technical content using a realistic business scenario and focuses on using Office as a decision-making tool.

The process of developing this unique series for you, the modern student or instructor, requires innovative ideas regarding the pedagogy and organization of the text. You learn best when doing—so you will be active from Page 1. Your learning goes to the next level when you are challenged to do more with less—your hand will be held at first but, progressively, the case exercises require more from you. Because you care about how things work in the real world—in your classes, your future jobs, your personal life—Real World Advice, Videos, and Success Stories are woven throughout the text. These innovative features will help you progress from a basic understanding of Office to mastery of each application, empowering you to perform with confidence in Windows 8, Word, Excel, Access, and PowerPoint, including on mobile devices.

No matter what career you may choose to pursue in life, this series will give you the foundation to succeed. **Your Office** uses cases that will enable you to be immersed in a realistic business as you learn Office in the context of a running business scenario—the Painted Paradise Resort & Spa. You will immediately delve into the many interesting, smaller businesses in this resort (golf course, spa, restaurants, hotel, etc.) to learn how a larger organization actually uses Office. You will learn how to make Office work for you now, as a student, and in your future career.

Today, the experience of working with Office is not isolated to working in a job in a cubicle. Your physical office is wherever you are with a laptop or a mobile device. Office has changed. It's modern. It's mobile. It's personal. And when you learn these valuable skills and master Office, you are able to make Office your own. The title of this series is a promise to you, the student: Our goal is to make Microsoft Office **Your Office**.

Key Features

- **Starting and Ending Files:** These appear before every case in the text. Starting Files identify exactly which Student Data Files are needed to complete each case. Ending Files are provided to show students the naming conventions they should use when saving their files. Each file icon is color coded by application.

- **Workshop Objectives List:** The learning objectives to be achieved as students work through the workshop. Page numbers are included for easy reference. These are revisited in the Concept Check at the end of the workshop.

- **Real World Success:** A boxed feature in the workshop opener that shares an anecdote from a real former student, describing how knowledge of Office has helped him or her to get ahead or be successful in his or her life.

- **Active Text Box:** Represents the active portion of the workshop and is easily distinguishable from explanatory text by the blue shaded background. Active Text helps students quickly identify what steps they need to follow to complete the workshop Prepare Case.

- **Quick Reference Box:** A boxed feature in the workshop, summarizing generic or alternative instructions on how to accomplish a task. This feature enables students to quickly find important skills.

- **Real World Advice Box:** A boxed feature in the workshop, offering advice and best practices for general use of important Office skills. The goal is to advise students as a manager might in a future job.

- **Side Note:** A brief tip or piece of information aligned visually with a step in the workshop, quickly providing key information to students completing that particular step.

- **Consider This:** In-text critical thinking questions and topics for discussion, set apart as a boxed feature, allowing students to step back from the project and think about the application of what they are learning and how these concepts might be used in the future.

- **Concept Check:** Review questions appearing at the end of the workshop, which require students to demonstrate their understanding of the objectives in that workshop.

- **Visual Summary:** A visual review of the objectives learned in the workshop using images from the completed solution file, mapped to the workshop objectives using callouts and page references so students can easily find the section of text to refer to for a refresher.

- **Business Application Icons:** Appear with every case in the text and clearly identify which business application students are being exposed to, i.e., Finance, Marketing, Operations, etc.

Business Application Icons

Customer Service

Finance & Accounting

General Business

Human Resources

Information Technology

Production & Operations

Sales & Marketing

Research & Development

Instructor Resources

The Instructor's Resource Center, available at www.pearsonhighered.com, includes the following:

- Prepared Exams with solution files for additional assessment.
- Annotated Solution Files with Scorecards assist with grading the Prepare, Practice, Problem Solve, and Perform Cases.
- Data and Solution Files.
- Rubrics for Perform Cases in Microsoft Word format enable instructors to easily grade open-ended assignments with no definite solution.
- PowerPoint Presentations with notes for each chapter.
- Instructor's Manual that provides detailed blueprints to achieve workshop learning objectives and outcomes and best use the unique structure of the modules.
- Complete Test Bank, also available in TestGen format.
- Syllabus templates.
- Additional Practice, Problem Solve, and Perform Cases to provide you with variety and choice in exercises both on the workshop and module levels.
- Scripted Lectures provide instructors with a lecture outline that mirrors the Workshop Prepare Case.
- Flexible, robust, and customizable content is available for all major online course platforms that include everything instructors need in one place. Please contact your sales representative for information on accessing course cartridges for WebCT or Blackboard.

Student Resources

- Companion Website
- Student Data Files

Pearson's Companion Website

www.pearsonhighered.com/youroffice offers expanded IT resources and downloadable supplements. Students can find the following self-study tools for each workshop:

- Online Workshop Review
- Workshop Objectives
- Glossary
- Student Data Files

Dear Students,

If you want an edge over the competition, make it personal. Whether you love sports, travel, the stock market, or ballet, your passion is personal to you. Capitalizing on your passion leads to success. You live in a global marketplace, and your competition is global. The honors students in China exceed the total number of students in North America. Skills can help set you apart, but passion will make you stand above. *Your Office* is the tool to harness your passion's true potential.

In prior generations, personalization in a professional setting was discouraged. You had a "work" life and a "home" life. As the Series Editor, I write to you about the vision for *Your Office* from my laptop, on my couch, in the middle of the night when inspiration strikes me. My classroom and living room are my office. Life has changed from generations before us.

So, let's get personal. My degrees are not in technology, but chemistry and law. I helped put myself through school by working full time in various jobs, including a successful technology consulting business that continues today. My generation did not grow up with computers, but I did. My father was a network administrator for the military. So, I was learning to program in Basic before anyone had played Nintendo's Duck Hunt or Tetris. Technology has always been one of my passions from a young age. In fact, I now tell my husband: don't buy me jewelry for my birthday, buy me the latest gadget on the market!

In my first law position, I was known as the Office guru to the extent that no one gave me a law assignment for the first two months. Once I submitted the assignment, my supervisor remarked, "Wow, you don't just know how to leverage technology, but you really know the law too." I can tell you novel-sized stories from countless prior students in countless industries who gained an edge from using Office as a tool. Bringing technology to your passion makes you well-rounded and a cut above the rest, no matter the industry or position.

I am most passionate about teaching, in particular teaching technology. I come from many generations of teachers, including my mother who is a kindergarten teacher. For over 12 years, I have found my dream job passing on my passion for teaching, technology, law, science, music, and life in general at the Kelley School of Business at Indiana University. I have tried to pass on the key to engaging passion to my students. I have helped them see what differentiates them from all the other bright students vying for the same jobs.

Microsoft Office is a tool. All of your competition will have learned Microsoft Office to some degree or another. Some will have learned it to an advanced level. Knowing Microsoft Office is important, but it is also fundamental. Without it, you will not be considered for a position.

Today, you step into your first of many future roles bringing Microsoft Office to your dream job working for Painted Paradise Resort & Spa. You will delve into the business side of the resort and learn how to use *Your Office* to maximum benefit.

Don't let the context of a business fool you. If you don't think of yourself as a business person, you have no need to worry. Whether you realize it or not, everything is business. If you want to be a nurse, you are entering the health care industry. If you want to be a football player in the NFL, you are entering the business of sports as entertainment. In fact, if you want to be a stay-at-home parent, you are entering the business of a family household where *Your Office* still gives you an advantage. For example, you will be able to prepare a budget in Excel and analyze what you need to do to afford a trip to Disney World!

At Painted Paradise Resort & Spa, you will learn how to make Office yours through four learning levels designed to maximize your understanding. You will Prepare, Practice, and Problem Solve your tasks. Then, you will astound when you Perform your new talents. You will be challenged through Consider This questions and gain insight through Real World Advice.

There is something more. You want success in what you are passionate about in your life. It is personal for you. In this position at Painted Paradise Resort & Spa, you will gain your personal competitive advantage that will stay with you for the rest of your life—*Your Office*.

Sincerely,

Amy Kinser

Series Editor

Painted Paradise

RESORT & SPA

Red Bluff Golf Course & Pro Shop

Turquoise Oasis Spa

Painted Treasures Gift Shop

Silver Moon Lounge

Event Planning & Catering

Indigo5 Restaurant

Welcome to the Team!

Welcome to your new office at Painted Paradise Resort & Spa, where we specialize in painting perfect getaways. As the Chief Technology Officer, I am excited to have staff dedicated to the Microsoft Office integration between all the areas of the resort. Our team is passionate about our paradise, and I hope you find this to be your dream position here!

Painted Paradise is a resort and spa in New Mexico catering to business people, romantics, families, and anyone who just needs to get away. Inside our resort are many distinct areas. Many of these areas operate as businesses in their own right but must integrate with the other areas of the resort. The main areas of the resort are as follows.

- The **Hotel** is overseen by our Chief Executive Officer, William Mattingly, and is at the core of our business. The hotel offers a variety of accommodations, ranging from individual rooms to a grand villa suite. Further, the hotel offers packages including spa, golf, and special events.

  Room rates vary according to size, season, demand, and discount. The hotel has discounts for typical groups, such as AARP. The hotel also has a loyalty program where guests can earn free nights based on frequency of visits. Guests may charge anything from the resort to the room.

- **Red Bluff Golf Course** is a private world-class golf course and pro shop. The golf course has services such as golf lessons from the famous golf pro John Schilling and playing packages. Also, the golf course attracts local residents. This requires variety in pricing schemes to accommodate both local and hotel guests. The pro shop sells many retail items online.

  The golf course can also be reserved for special events and tournaments. These special events can be in conjunction with a wedding, conference, meetings, or other event covered by the event planning and catering area of the resort.

- **Turquoise Oasis Spa** is a full-service spa. Spa services include haircuts, pedicures, massages, facials, body wraps, waxing, and various other spa services—typical to exotic. Further, the spa offers private consultation, weight training (in the fitness center), a water bar, meditation areas, and steam rooms. Spa services are offered both in the spa and in the resort guest's room.

  Turquoise Oasis Spa uses top-of-the-line products and some house-brand products. The retail side offers products ranging from candles to age-defying home treatments. These products can also be purchased online. Many of the hotel guests who fall in love with the house-brand soaps, lotions, candles, and other items appreciate being able to buy more at any time.

  The spa offers a multitude of packages including special hotel room packages that include spa treatments. Local residents also use the spa. So, the spa guests are not limited to hotel guests. Thus, the packages also include pricing attractive to the local community.

3355 Hemmingway Circle • Santa Fe, New Mexico 89566

- **Painted Treasures Gift Shop** has an array of items available for purchase, from toiletries to clothes to presents for loved ones back home including a healthy section of kids' toys for traveling business people. The gift shop sells a small sampling from the spa, golf course pro shop, and local New Mexico culture. The gift shop also has a small section of snacks and drinks. The gift shop has numerous part-time employees including students from the local college.

- **The Event Planning & Catering** area is central to attracting customers to the resort. From weddings to conferences, the resort is a popular destination. The resort has a substantial number of staff dedicated to planning, coordinating, setting up, catering, and maintaining these events. The resort has several facilities that can accommodate large groups. Packages and prices vary by size, room, and other services such as catering. Further, the Event Planning & Catering team works closely with local vendors for floral decorations, photography, and other event or wedding typical needs. However, all catering must go through the resort (no outside catering permitted). Lastly, the resort stocks several choices of decorations, table arrangements, and centerpieces. These range from professional, simple, themed, and luxurious.

- **Indigo5** and the **Silver Moon Lounge**, a world-class restaurant and lounge that is overseen by the well-known Chef Robin Sanchez. The cuisine is balanced and modern. From steaks to pasta to local southwestern meals, Indigo5 attracts local patrons in addition to resort guests. While the catering function is separate from the restaurant—though menu items may be shared—the restaurant does support all room service for the resort. The resort also has smaller food venues onsite such as the Terra Cotta Brew coffee shop in the lobby.

Currently, these areas are using Office to various degrees. In some areas, paper and pencil are still used for most business functions. Others have been lucky enough to have some technology savvy team members start Microsoft Office Solutions.

Using your skills, I am confident that you can help us integrate and use Microsoft Office on a whole new level! I hope you are excited to call Painted Paradise Resort & Spa *Your Office*.

Looking forward to working with you more closely!

Aidan Matthews

Aidan Matthews
Chief Technology Officer

WORKSHOP 1 | PLAN A PROJECT

Prepare Case

Painted Paradise Golf Resort – First Annual Charity Golf Tournament

The Painted Paradise Golf Resort will be holding its first annual charity golf tournament to raise money for the purchase of textbooks to be donated to the elementary

©basketman23/Fotolia

schools in Santa Fe, New Mexico. The VP of special projects, Julie Rholfing, has assigned Patti Rochelle, the tournament-planning manager, to be the project manager of this event. Julie has asked Patti to use Microsoft Project 2013 to begin planning this tournament. Before Patti can begin entering in the tasks that need to be completed for the tournament, she must first understand the Project 2013 window, Project 2013 views, and the Project 2013 calendar. You will help Patti get started with the setup of this project.

REAL WORLD SUCCESS

"As a Project Analyst, I used Project 2013 on a regular basis to ensure all tasks were on track. However, because I had never had any formal training, it was an overly manual effort to schedule and update activities, along with generating reports. After learning to use Project 2013, I now know several short cuts on how to better utilize the software. I would recommend this software to anyone involved in managing projects."

—Lacey, project management student

Student data file needed for this workshop:

 No data file needed

You will save your file as:

 pm01ws01CharityGolfTournament_LastFirst.mpp

Preparing a Project Plan

It is common today to work with teams or with groups of people to reach a desired outcome. Outcomes can be reached by brainstorming, communicating, planning, and then completing the plan as defined. Whether you work on a team or work alone, taking the time to plan before acting may help improve your chances of success. The process of planning and following through with a plan is project management.

In this workshop, you will be introduced to project management terminology and processes. Then you will learn to use Project 2013, a project planning software often used to help create detailed project plans.

Understand Project Management and Microsoft Project Terminology

Project management is a process of initiating, planning, executing, monitoring, and closing a project's tasks and resources in order to accomplish a project's goal. **A project goal** is the desired result of a project upon completion. A project's goal is met when project tasks are completed on time, on budget, and within the scope of a given project. All projects, large or small, should follow the project management process groups, as shown in Table 1, to reach project success.

Process Group	Responsibility
Initiating	Set a project goal; identify a project schedule; define a project budget
Planning	Enter project tasks; determine task relationships; assign project resources
Executing	Produce results; report results
Monitoring and Control	Update tasks as in progress or completed; manage resources
Closing	Analyze performance; prepare final reports

Table 1 Project management process groups

REAL WORLD ADVICE **Resources for Project Managers**

If you are new to project management, you are not alone! There are many resources available for project managers who seek assistance with project management information and practices. One resource is *A Guide to the Project Management Body of Knowledge (PMBOK® Guide)*. This guide defines project management terminology and presents industry standard guidelines for managing projects.

Another resource is the Project Management Institute (PMI). By joining PMI, project managers can get access to PMI publications, be kept updated on global standards, have networking opportunities with other project managers, and have access to project management tools and templates to help manage projects. PMI also provides training and access to the Project Management Professional (PMP) certification.

Office.microsoft.com offers videos on Project 2013. This is a helpful resource for project managers who may be new to using the software.

A **project manager** is the person responsible for overseeing all the details of the project plan. The project manager works to create a plan that will lead to project success.

A project manager also motivates project team members to achieve the project goals. Project managers may choose to use project planning software such as Project 2013 to help them plan and achieve project success. Project planning software keeps track of tasks, the duration to complete tasks, scheduled dates, project resources, and project costs organized in one location for a more efficient way of managing a project. It is a tool that allows project managers to track, analyze, and summarize project information.

In order to use project planning software, it is important to understand terminology associated with the software. A **task** is an activity that is completed to reach a project goal. For example, when planning for a charity golf tournament, a task could be "set tournament date and time" or "prepare preliminary budget."

Task duration is how long you predict it will take to complete a task. Task durations in Project can be entered in minutes, hours, days, weeks, months, and years. For example, you may determine it takes two days to "set tournament date and time" but two weeks to "prepare preliminary budget."

A **predecessor task** is a task that must be completed before the next task can start. A task that has a predecessor is called a **successor task**. Project managers often use the term task dependency when referring to how the predecessor or successor tasks are connected. A **task dependency** is a relationship between two tasks that defines which task(s) have to finish before the next task(s) can start. A task dependency is often called a task link.

Since not all tasks are the same in a project, scheduling them the same way may not be an option. Therefore, some tasks may have constraints applied. A **constraint** is a limitation set on a task. For example, a task of "create tournament website" may have a constraint of "finish no later than" a certain date to ensure the website is up and running in time to gather enough registrations for the event. Constraints on tasks affect how the task is scheduled. Setting constraints on tasks will determine how Project 2013 will schedule a task. Besides setting specific date constraints on a task, the following task constraints can be set on an individual task:

- As late as possible
- As soon as possible
- Finish no earlier than
- Finish no later than
- Must finish on
- Must start on
- Start no earlier than
- Start no later than

A **resource** is a work, material, or cost associated with a project task. **Work resources** are people and equipment. **Material resources** are resources consumed during the project. **Cost resources** are independent costs you want to associate with a task. For example, a task of "provide transportation from the airport" may have a cost of "$2,000 limousine service." Project managers assign resources to project tasks to help determine a project's schedule and a project's cost.

The **scope** of a project is what must be completed to deliver a specific product or service. The project scope includes the meeting of project goals, tasks, and deadlines set. Project managers use planning software such as Project 2013 to prevent deviating from the scope of a project.

A **milestone** is a task that is used to communicate project progress or mark a significant point in a project such as the end of a project phase. For example, a milestone for the charity golf tournament could be "tournament website goes live". Milestones are entered into the Project 2013 software as a task with zero duration. By default, Project 2013 displays a milestone as a diamond in the Gantt chart. A **Gantt chart** is a graphical representation of the tasks listed in the Entry table.

Starting a Project

You have been asked to work on the planning team for the Painted Paradise Golf Resort Charity Golf Tournament. Your role on the team will be to set up the project plan in Project 2013. To get started, you will open and save a project.

PM1.00 To Begin, Save, Close, and Open a Project

a. Click the **Start Screen** or desktop, and then start typing **proj**. The Search box will appear at the right-hand side of your screen and Project 2013 will appear in the Apps list on the left-hand side of your screen.

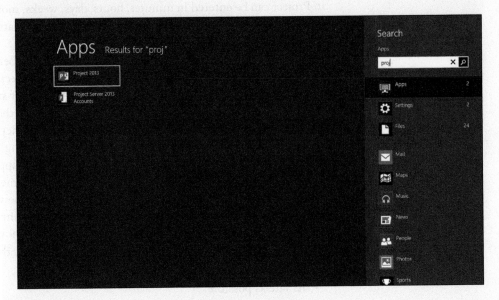

Figure 1   Windows Start Screen with Project 2013 Search

b. Click **Project 2013** in the search results. The Project Start screen is displayed.

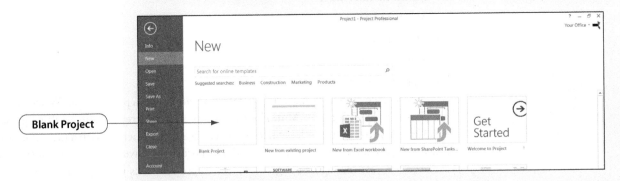

Figure 2   Creating a new Project

c. Click **Blank Project** to open a new blank project.

d. Click the **FILE** tab, and then click **Save As**. Click **Computer**.

Figure 3 Save As screen

e. Click **Browse**, and then navigate to the location where you are saving your files.

f. Click in the File name box, type pm01ws01CharityGolfTournament_LastFirst, using your last name and first name. Click **Save**.

g. Click the **FILE** tab, and then click **Close**. The project file will close but the MS Project application will remain open.

h. In the Navigation Pane click **Open**, and then browse for **pm01ws01CharityGolfTournament_LastFirst.mpp**. Click **pm01ws01CharityGolfTournament_LastFirst.mpp**, and then click **Open** to reopen your project file.

> **Troubleshooting**
>
> If Project 2013 closed completely, perform steps a-c again. Click the FILE tab, and then click Open. Browse to where you store your files, and then click pm01ws01CharityGolfTournament_LastFirst.mpp. Click Open.

Explore the Project 2013 Window

When opening a new Project 2013 file, the default view is the Gantt Chart view as shown in Figure 4. (There may be slight differences with the view of your Project 2013 window. You will learn how to adjust the Project 2013 window in this workshop.)

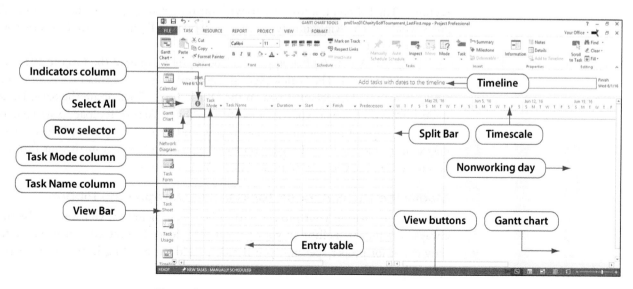

Figure 4 Project 2013 window

Gantt Chart view includes the Gantt chart and the Entry table. In the Gantt chart, a project's tasks are shown against a timeline. The activities are displayed as horizontal bars in which the length of the bar is determined by the duration of the activities and start/finish dates. The **Entry table** is used to enter task information and is located to the left of the Gantt chart. The Entry table contains columns and rows similar to Microsoft Excel 2013. The Entry table is used to record project tasks, durations, predecessors, and resources. Each task becomes a new row in the Entry table. A vertical **split bar** separates the Entry table and the Gantt chart. If desired, you can drag the split bar to resize the panes.

A **row selector** is the box containing the row number of a task in the Entry table. The **Select All** button is a button that selects all task and task information in the Entry table.

The **Timeline** is a visual representation of the project from start to finish. The Timeline is displayed above the Entry table and Gantt chart and below the Ribbon. You can choose what to display on the Timeline. If the Timeline is added, it will be visible in the Project 2013 views as well. The **timescale** is located above the Gantt chart. The timescale displays the unit of measure that determines the length of the Gantt bars in the Gantt chart.

The light gray vertical bars in the Gantt chart represent nonworking days. A **nonworking day** is a day during which Project 2013 will not schedule work to occur. Therefore, if a task starts at 8:00 A.M. on a Friday and has a three-day duration, Project 2013 would schedule the task for Friday 8:00 A.M.–5:00 P.M., Monday 8:00 A.M.–5:00 P.M., and Tuesday 8:00 A.M.–5:00 P.M.

The **Indicators column** is a column in the Entry table that will display an icon that provides further information about a task. For example, if the constraint of a specific date is set to a task, a calendar icon would appear in the Indicators column.

The **Task Mode column** indicates the mode in which Project 2013 will schedule tasks, either manually or automatically. A task's mode can be adjusted by using the Task Mode arrow within the Task Mode column.

The **Task Name column** is a location in the Entry table where the name of each task is entered. One task is entered per row. Task names should be descriptive but not too wordy.

The **View Bar** is a vertical bar on the left-hand side of the Project 2013 window that contains buttons for quick access to different Project 2013 views. The View Bar can be turned on and off based on a project planner's preference. You can use the View Bar's navigation buttons to navigate within the different Project 2013 views.

Project 2013 uses the Office 2013 design and layout of the Ribbon as shown in Figure 4. The Ribbon is a row of tabs with buttons that appears at the top of the Project 2013 window. The Ribbon may be open as shown in Figure 4 or may also be collapsed to save screen space.

The Quick Access Toolbar appears in the top-left corner of the Project 2013 window as shown in Figure 4. The **Quick Access Toolbar** is a series of small icons for commonly used commands. The default icons on the Quick Access Toolbar are the Save, Undo, and Redo buttons. However, you can modify the Quick Access Toolbar to fit your project needs by adding or removing buttons. If you often print reports from Project 2013, you may want to add the Print Preview button. If you often have to e-mail your Project 2013 files to colleagues, you may want to add the Email button.

Modify the Quick Access Toolbar and Collapse the Ribbon

Since you are sharing your project with other team members, you want to be sure you always have proper spelling in your project plan. Since Project 2013 does not automatically check for proper spelling, you decide to add the Spelling button to your project's Quick Access Toolbar.

PM1.01 **To Modify the Quick Access Toolbar and Collapse the Ribbon**

a. Click the **Quick Access Toolbar** arrow, and then click **More Commands**.

Figure 5   Quick Access Toolbar shortcut menu

b. Click the **Choose commands from** arrow.

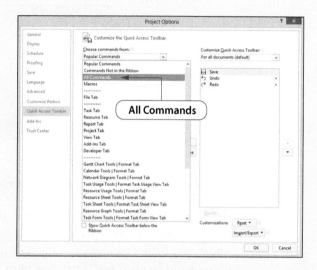

Figure 6   Project Options dialog box to customize the Quick Access Toolbar

SIDE NOTE

Modifying the Quick Access Toolbar
You can also add buttons to the Quick Access Toolbar by right-clicking a button on the Ribbon and clicking **Add to Quick Access Toolbar**.

c. Click **All Commands** and then scroll through the list of commands. Click **Spelling**, and then click **Add**.

d. Click **OK**. The Spelling button will be added to the Quick Access Toolbar.

Figure 7   Modified Quick Access Toolbar

e. Double-click the **TASK** tab. Notice the Ribbon is now collapsed.

Figure 8   Ribbon collapsed

f.   Double-click the **TASK** tab again to show the Ribbon.

g.   Right-click the **TASK** tab. Click **Collapse the Ribbon**. The Ribbon is now collapsed.

h.   Right-click the **TASK** tab again. Click **Collapse the Ribbon** to show the Ribbon.

i.   On the Quick Access Toolbar, click **Save** 🖫.

Prepare a Project Schedule

Project 2013 has a complex scheduling engine, so to understand how it will calculate a project's schedule, it is important to review the Project Information dialog box. The Project Information button 🔳 is found in the Properties group of the Project tab. Click the Project Information button to open the Project Information dialog box.

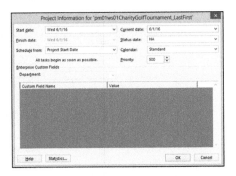

Figure 9   Project Information dialog box

The **Project Information dialog box** is used to update various aspects of a project such as the project's start date or finish date, current date, status date, project base calendar, etc. Before entering specific task information for a project, the project's information should be identified. First, one must select whether the project will be scheduled from Start date or from Finish date. Project **Start date** is the date Project 2013 will use to begin scheduling tasks to calculate the Finish date. Project **Finish date** is the date Project 2013 will use to begin scheduling tasks to calculate the Start date. A project can only be scheduled by Start date or Finish date, not by both. Start date is the default in the software.

If a project is set to calculate by Start date, as shown in Figure 9, all tasks will be scheduled to begin as soon as possible. If you schedule by Start date, Project 2013 will calculate when the project should finish. The Finish date would be determined by individual tasks, task durations, task predecessors, and resources assigned to tasks.

If a project is set to calculate by Finish date, all tasks will be scheduled to begin as late as possible, as shown in Figure 10. If the project is scheduled by Finish date, Project 2013 will determine the date you must begin your project to be able to complete the project by the set finish date. The Start date would be determined by individual tasks, task durations, task predecessors, and resources assigned to tasks.

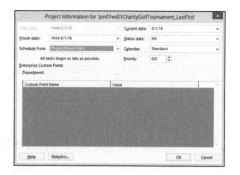

Figure 10   Project scheduled by Finish date

The **Current date** is today's date as determined by your computer's clock. You can easily change the current date by entering a new date in the current date section of the Project Information dialog box or by clicking the arrow for Current date and selecting a new date.

The **Status date** is the date you set to run reports on a project's progress. For example, if you have a weekly team meeting on Monday morning to review the current status of the project for the week ahead, you may set the Status date to the Friday before the Monday morning meeting. To run status reports, a project baseline must be set. A **baseline** is a record of each task at a point in time from which you will track project progress.

Project 2013 determines a project's schedule off the base calendar. A base calendar is the calendar applied to the project in the Project Information dialog box and provides a template for how the software will schedule tasks and resources. The default base calendar is the **Standard calendar.** The Standard calendar specifies hours in which work can occur. These hours are referred to as working time. If a project is set to schedule based on the Standard calendar, all tasks and each resource are scheduled according to this calendar. The Standard calendar is based on a 40-hour work week with an 8-hour work day (8:00 A.M. to 12:00 P.M. and 1:00 P.M. to 5:00 P.M.) Monday through Friday. Saturday and Sunday are considered nonworking days. If you recall, nonworking days are days that Project 2013 will not schedule any work to be completed.

Other available predetermined calendar choices are the Night Shift calendar as shown in Figure 11. The **24 Hours calendar** assigns a schedule with continuous work. This type of calendar may be assigned to a project that must work around the clock—for example, a mechanical process. The **Night Shift calendar** assigns a schedule that is sometimes referred to as the "graveyard" shift schedule of Monday night through Saturday morning, 11:00 P.M. to 8:00 A.M., with an hour off for break.

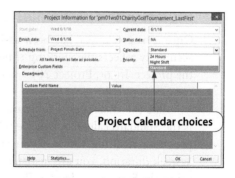

Figure 11   Project Calendar choices

Project manager's can set the priority of a project in the Project Information dialog box. The priority of a project is determined on a scale of 1 to 1,000 with 1 being the least priority and 1,000 being the most priority. A project with a priority of 1,000 is considered more important than a project with a priority of 100. Priorities are only used when project managers are trying to balance resource assignments among tasks and projects.

Preparing a Project Schedule Using the Project Information Dialog Box

To be sure the project information is accurate for the needs of the charity golf tournament project, project manager Patti Rochelle asks you to set the project schedule to Finish date and to set the finish date to the tournament's date of June 18, 2016.

PM1.02 To Change the Project Information

a. Click the **PROJECT** tab, and then click **Project Information** ⊡.

SIDE NOTE

Selecting Finish Date
You can also type in a project's finish date versus scrolling through the calendar.

b. Click the **Schedule from:** arrow, and then click **Project Finish Date** to change the project to schedule by Finish date.

c. Click the **Finish date** arrow. Scroll through the calendar until you see June 2016. Click **June 18, 2016**.

d. Click the **Current date** arrow. Scroll through the calendar and click **December 1, 2015**.

e. Verify the **Standard Calendar** is the selected calendar.

Figure 12 Project Information dialog box

f. Click **OK**.

g. Click **Save** 🖫 or click the **FILE** tab, and then click **Save**. Do not close your Project 2013 file.

Modify a Project Calendar

Once a base calendar has been assigned to a project, it is important the base calendar accurately reflects the working time hours a project team is actually available to work on the project. If not, Project 2013 will calculate an incorrect project schedule that may lead to a project's failure.

Take the charity golf tournament as an example. If the base calendar of the project is the Standard calendar, you are telling Project 2013 all tasks are assigned to a 40-hour per week working time. If you enter a task of "prepare preliminary budget" with a 1-week duration, you are instructing Project 2013 to schedule 40 hours to this task. If using the Standard calendar, Project 2013 will assign this task a duration of 5 working days (8 hours per day for 5 days for a total of 40 hours).

Now imagine there are only 20 hours available each week to dedicate to this project due to other commitments (not the 40 hours as set by the base Standard calendar). If this is the case, the Standard calendar must be modified to reflect the actual working time available. If modifications to the calendar are not made, Project 2013 will schedule the work incorrectly. To review how Project 2013 schedules tasks based on a project's calendar, refer to Table 2.

Calendar	Duration	Working Time
Standard Calendar with a 40-hour work week	1 week duration = 40 hours of work	5 days (40 hours/8 hours per day = 5 days)
Modified Standard Calendar with a 20-hour work week	1 week duration = 40 hours of work	10 days (40 hours/4 hours per day = 10 days)

Table 2 Duration and start or finish dates

Modifying a Project Calendar

It is possible to adjust the Standard calendar to meet your project needs. Patti Rochelle, the project manager for the charity golf tournament, and her project team are only available to work on this project Tuesday through Friday 8:00 A.M. to 12:00 P.M. (16 hours per week). You will need to adjust the base Standard calendar to reflect the actual working time available.

PM1.03 To Change the Project Calendar Working Time

a. Click the **PROJECT** tab, if necessary.

b. In the Properties group, click **Change Working Time** to open the Change Working Time dialog box for the Standard calendar.

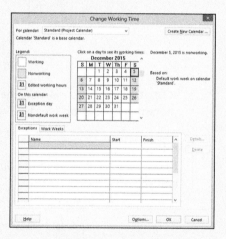

Figure 13   Change Working Time dialog box

> **Troubleshooting**
> If your calendar in the Change Working Time dialog box is showing a different date, scroll through the calendar until you see December 1, 2015.

c. Click the **Work Weeks** tab in the bottom section of the dialog box, and then click the **Details** button to open the Details for dialog box.

Figure 14   Calendar Details dialog box

d. In the Details for dialog box click **Monday**, and then click **Set days to nonworking time**.

Figure 15   Mondays set to nonworking days

e. Click **Tuesday**, press and hold [Shift], and then click **Friday**.

f. Click **Set day(s) to these specific working times**.

g. Click **2** in Row 2 in the specific work times grid, and then press [Delete] to clear the 1:00 P.M.–5:00 P.M. work times.

Figure 16   Specific working times set for working days

h. Click **OK**. The base calendar has now been changed to reflect that Mondays are nonworking days and Tuesday–Friday working hours are 8:00 A.M. to 12:00 P.M.

> **Troubleshooting**
> If necessary, scroll through the calendar in the Change Working Time dialog box until you see December 2015.

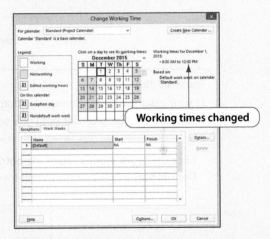

Figure 17   Change Working Time dialog box with working time changes set

i. Click **OK** to close the Change Working Time dialog box, and then click **Save** [⊞].

REAL WORLD ADVICE | **Working with Microsoft Project 2013 Around the Globe**

In today's global economy, it is likely you will work for a company that has locations in different states or even countries. Therefore, when preparing your project calendar, consideration must be given to where your project team members reside. Although many countries consider a typical work week Monday through Friday with Saturday and Sunday as nonworking days, some countries may work on a 6-day work week or even a 4-day work week. So that Project 2013 has accurate information when creating a project's schedule, it is important that the base calendar accurately reflects the availability of all project team members.

Adding Exceptions to the Project Calendar

Since organizations do not all observe the same holidays, Project 2013 does not include any holidays in the Project 2013 calendars. If your organization and/or project team observes holidays, you should account for them in the project's calendar. If holidays are not accounted for, Project 2013 cannot factor them into the project's schedule and therefore may miscalculate the project schedule by assigning work on a nonworking day. Holidays can be added to a project calendar by creating Exceptions to a project's base calendar.

Patti Rochelle, the project manager for the charity golf tournament, has clarified that the following holidays will be observed by the project staff: December 24–25, 2015; January 1, 2016; and March 24–25, 2016. Therefore, you will need to make these days nonworking days in the project's calendar by adding exceptions to the project's calendar.

PM1.04 To Add an Exception to the Project Calendar

a. Click the **PROJECT** tab, if necessary, and then in the Properties group click **Change Working Time** to open the Change Working Time dialog box once again.

b. On the calendar, click **December 24, 2015**, press and hold Shift and click **December 25, 2015**. Both days are selected.

> **Troubleshooting**
>
> If you do not see the correct dates on the Change Working Time calendar, you may need to scroll through the calendar until December 2015 is visible.

c. In the bottom section of the Change Working Time dialog box, click the **Exceptions** tab, if necessary, and then click in the first empty cell in the **Name** column.

d. Enter Holiday break as the first Exception, and then press Tab. Click in the next blank row of the Exceptions table. Verify December 24–25, 2015 has been changed to nonworking days.

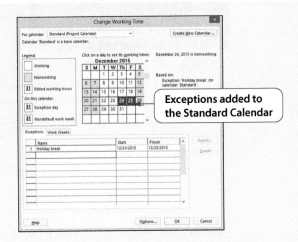

Figure 18 Holiday break calendar exception added

e. Click in the next empty cell in the **Exceptions Name** column and enter New Year's break.

f. Press Tab, and then click in the **Start** column.

g. Click the **Start** column arrow to display the date picker, change the Start date to **January 1, 2016**, and then press Tab. Click in the Finish column to verify January 1 is set to a nonworking day.

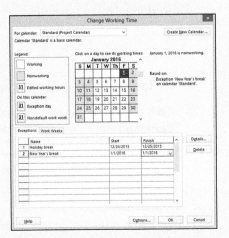

Figure 19 New Year's break calendar exception added

> **Troubleshooting**
> If an exception is not appearing as a nonworking day in the calendar, click the Exception row in the Exceptions Name box, and then click the Details button. Set the selected Exception day to Nonworking, and then click OK.

h. Repeat steps e-g for the following exception: Spring break, **March 24-25, 2016**. Click in the next blank row of the Exceptions table to verify the spring break dates are non-working days.

i. Click **OK** to close the Change Working Time dialog box, and then click **Save** ⊞, leaving your project file open.

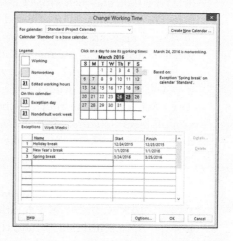

Figure 20   Change Working Time calendar exceptions added

REAL WORLD ADVICE   Task Calendars

One size does not fit all when it comes to Project 2013 calendars! To make sure Project 2013 is creating an accurate schedule, individual tasks may need to be completed outside of the base calendar working time. For example, if the charity golf tournament's base calendar is set to working times of Tuesday–Friday, 8:00 A.M. to 12:00 P.M., but training for event staff needs to occur from 1:00 P.M. to 5:00 P.M., a task calendar can be created to reflect the training times of 1:00 P.M. to 5:00 P.M. Once a task calendar is created, it is applied to the appropriate task(s), and Project 2013 is then able to schedule those particular tasks outside of the base calendar working times. Task Calendars can be created for any task that does not follow the working and nonworking times set on the project's base calendar.

QUICK REFERENCE   Creating a Task Calendar

To create a task calendar click the Project tab, and then:

1. Click Change Working Time in the Properties group.
2. Click the Create New Calendar button, and then enter a name for the task calendar. Click OK.
3. Click the Work Weeks tab.
4. Click the next empty cell in the Name column. Enter a descriptive name and press ⌈Tab⌉, and then click in the Start cell.
5. Click the Details button. In the Details dialog box, choose the appropriate option for your task calendar. Edit the From and To times as necessary. Click OK in both dialog boxes.

   Once the new task calendar is created, it would need to be assigned to specific tasks using the Task Information dialog box.

Understand Manually Scheduled Versus Auto Scheduled Projects

To understand how Project 2013 is scheduling tasks, it is important to identify if tasks are being scheduled manually or automatically. The default in Project 2013 is for tasks to be **Manually Scheduled**. In this mode, you enter a task duration and the task Start date for a task, and then Project 2013 will calculate the Finish date. In other words, task dates are not calculated or adjusted by Project's 2013 scheduling engine, even if changes to related tasks are made. Project managers who desire more control over the project schedule may elect to use manual scheduling.

If a project manager wants to take advantage of Project's 2013 scheduling engine, however, the project would likely be set to Auto Scheduled. If a project is set to **Auto Scheduled**, the project schedule is calculated based on the project's calendar, project tasks and task durations, task dependencies, resource assignments, and any constraint dates assigned to tasks. Auto scheduled projects are more structured than manually scheduled projects.

Figure 21 displays how Project 2013 is scheduling the two tasks differently. Because Task 1 is being manually scheduled, it has no Start date or Finish date calculated by Project 2013 even though a duration of two days has been assigned to the task. Task 2 is set to Auto Scheduled and therefore the Start date and Finish date are calculated by Project 2013 based on the project's calendar and the task duration. Also note the differences in the Gantt bars in the Gantt chart from Manually Scheduled to Auto Scheduled tasks.

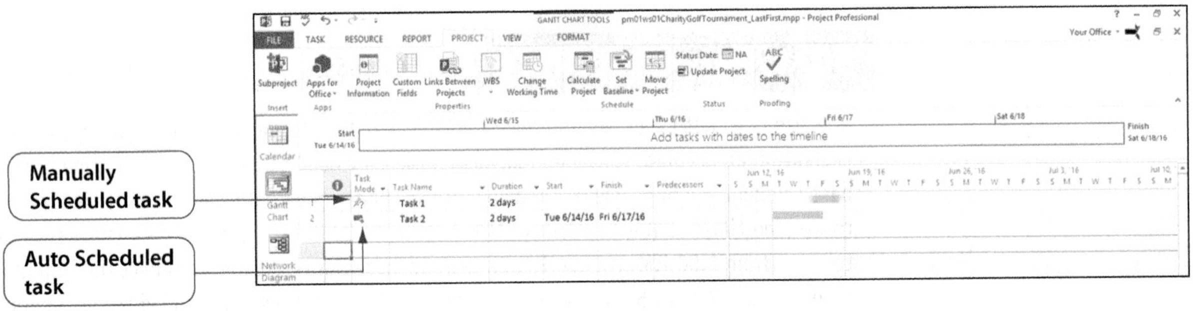

Figure 21 Manually Scheduled versus Auto Scheduled tasks

Table 3 displays several differences in scheduling a project manually versus automatically:

	Manual Scheduling	Automatic Scheduling
Duration	Can be number, date, or text information, such as "4 days" or "a few days"	Only numbers can be used that represent length and units, such as "4 days" or "2 weeks"
Project Calendar	Ignored by Project	Used by Project to determine a project's schedule
Constraints	Ignored by Project	Used by Project to determine task Start or Finish date
Task Relationships (links)	Can be assigned but won't change the task schedule	Can be assigned and will change the schedule of a task
Resources	Can be assigned to tasks but won't change the task schedule	Can be assigned to tasks. Used by Project to Help determine best schedule

Table 3 Manual scheduling vs. automatic scheduling

Auto Scheduling a Project

A project can be set to Auto Scheduled so that all tasks, unless otherwise specified, are scheduled by Project's scheduling engine. If a project is set to Auto Scheduled, individual tasks can be changed to Manually Scheduled, if necessary. A project set to Manually Scheduled will allow the project manager to determine the Start and Finish dates of a project's tasks. If a project is set to Manually Scheduled, individual tasks can be set to

Auto Scheduled. To change individual tasks, click the Task tab and click Auto Schedule from the Tasks group or click the arrow in the Task Mode column.

You are asked to set the project to Auto Scheduled so that Project 2013 can help you determine when you must start this project in order to finish by the tournament date of June 18, 2016.

PM1.05 To Set a Project to Auto Scheduled

a. Click **NEW TASKS: MANUALLY SCHEDULED** on the status bar.

Figure 22 Project Status Bar

b. Click **Auto Scheduled - Task dates are calculated by Microsoft Project**. All tasks will now be calculated by Project 2013 unless set individually to Manually Scheduled.

c. Click **Save** 🖫.

Creating a Project Plan

Understanding project management terminology, exploring the Project 2013 window, adjusting the Project 2013 calendar, and choosing a scheduling method is just the start to creating a project plan. Time also needs to be spent on identifying project tasks, task durations, task dependencies, and task constraints.

Identify Project Tasks

Tasks are activities that must be completed to accomplish a project goal. Tasks are entered into the Entry table in Gantt Chart view but can also be entered in the Network Diagram view and the Calendar view. Task names should be concise, and each task should be entered on a separate row in the Entry table. Tasks are assigned durations by the project's manager. In Project 2013, the default for a duration of one day is eight hours. Even if the project schedule is set to a 20-hour work week versus a 40-hour work week, Project 2013 still calculates one day as eight hours by default.

Durations help Project 2013 to calculate a task's Start (or Finish) date if a project is set to Auto Scheduled. Durations can be entered into the software using the following abbreviations:

QUICK REFERENCE	Entering Task Durations
Duration Abbreviation	**Result Duration**
1 min	1 minute
1 h	1 hour
1 d	1 day (default) or 8 hours
1 w	1 week
1 mon	1 month

Each task in a project is unique from other tasks within the same project, even if the tasks are related in some way. Information about a single task can be found in the Task Information dialog box by selecting the Information button on the Task tab. The **Task Information** dialog box includes all the details for a single task. Project managers can use the Task Information dialog box to view and update task details such as resource assignments, predecessors, and task calendar. Information for a task is divided into six categories (tabs): General, Predecessors, Resources, Advanced, Notes, and Custom Fields as shown in Figure 23. You can also use the Task Information dialog box to make changes to a task.

Figure 23   Task Information dialog box

Task names should be brief. Therefore, more information may need to be added to a task for clarification. This can be done with a task **Note**. A task Note acts as a sticky note for a task and can be added on the Notes tab in the Task Information dialog box. A note can provide more information on a task such as a web link, a phone number, or even an embedded file, such as an Excel spreadsheet, that provides further information on the task.

Navigating around an Entry table uses keystrokes similar to those used in other Microsoft applications.

QUICK REFERENCE	Navigating the Entry Table
Keyboard Shortcut	**Moves the Active Cell**
Enter	Down one row in same column
Shift + Enter	Up one row in same column
Home	First column of the current row
End	Last column of the current row
Ctrl + Home	First column and row
Ctrl + End	Last column of the last row
PageUp	Up one screen
PageDown	Down one screen
Tab	One column to right
Shift + Tab	One column to left

Entering Project Tasks

Now that you have prepared your project plan by adjusting the project calendar, and setting the project to schedule automatically and by finish date, you are ready to create your project plan. Patti Rochelle, the charity golf tournament-planning manager, has given you a list of tasks to enter into the project's Entry table.

To Enter Project Tasks

SIDE NOTE
Text Wrap
Project 2013 has a Wrap
Text feature for task names.
If the name is longer than
the column, the text will
wrap within the cell.

a. Click in the **Task Name** cell in row 1. Enter the task name Set tournament objectives.

b. Press Tab. The default value of 1 day? will appear in the Duration column.

Figure 24 Entry table with new task default duration

SIDE NOTE
Task Schedule
The task is scheduled to
start on June 16, 2016
because the project is
scheduling by Finish
date so all tasks will be
scheduled to start *As Late
As Possible*.

c. Enter **6h** in the Duration column. Press Tab. Notice how Project 2013 assigns a Start date and Finish date because your project is set to Auto Scheduled. The task is scheduled over two days because there are only 4 hours available in a day to complete a task. Note the Auto Scheduled symbol 🖥️ in the Task Mode column.

Auto Scheduled symbol

Figure 25 Entry table with new task and task duration added

SIDE NOTE
Project-Scheduled Changes
Whenever changes are
made to affect a start or
finish date of a task(s),
those dates will be
highlighted with a blue
background.

d. With **Set tournament objectives** (Task 1) selected, click the **TASK** tab, and then in the Properties group, click **Information** 🖥️ to open the Task Information dialog box. Explore the various tabs that can contain information about **Set tournament objectives**. Click **Cancel**.

e. Enter the remaining tasks below in the Entry table. Remember you can use abbreviations for the durations.

SIDE NOTE
Task Information
You can also open the Task
Information dialog box by
double-clicking a task.

Task	Task Name	Task Duration
2	Determine project team	4 hours
3	Set tournament date and time	1 day
4	Prepare preliminary budget	6 hours
5	Create tournament website	2 weeks
6	Solicit potential tournament sponsors	1 week
7	Select tournament sponsors	4 hours
8	Solicit celebrity appearances	3 weeks
9	Create volunteer list	4 hours
10	Sign contract agreement	1 hour

f. Click **Save** 🔲.

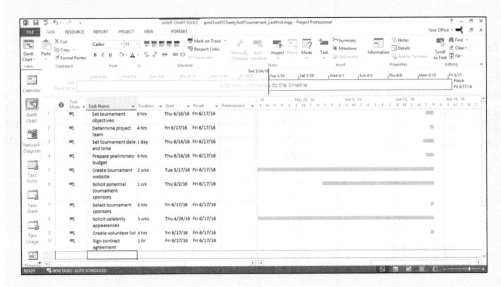

Figure 26 Entry table with tasks added

CONSIDER THIS | **Task Duration**

Why is a task duration of one day being assigned a calendar duration of two days? The Project calendar for the charity golf tournament was adjusted to a 4-hour working day of 8:00 A.M. to 12:00 P.M. Therefore, by entering in a duration of 1d (one day = 8 hours) Project scheduled the task to be completed over two calendar days: 4 available hours on day one, and 4 available hours on day two. Is using the day duration confusing? Consider entering durations in hours instead.

All the tasks are set to end on the actual tournament date. The schedule is set that way for now because your project is scheduled by Finish date and all tasks are scheduled to start *As Late As Possible*. Project tasks will push ahead in time as you create a more detailed project schedule later this workshop.

Modify Project Tasks in Project 2013

Project 2013 makes it easy to edit a project plan by adding, deleting, or changing existing tasks. As you are planning your project, you may discover that you need to add an additional task(s) in the middle of your project plan. Project 2013 allows tasks to be inserted by using the Ribbon, the shortcut menu, or the keyboard. Inserting a task in the middle of a project plan is similar to adding a row in Excel 2013 because Project 2013 will push every subsequent task down one row and adjust the project accordingly.

Adding and Modifying Project Tasks in the Entry Table

After brainstorming at a team meeting, the charity golf tournament planning team has identified a few additional tasks to be added to the project plan as well as an adjustment to task durations. You will add these tasks.

PM1.07 To Modify a Task List

SIDE NOTE

Adding Tasks in the Entry Table

Similar to Excel 2013, new task rows are added above the active row.

a. Click any cell in task row 4, **Prepare preliminary budget**, and then click the **TASK** tab, if necessary. In the Insert group, click the **Task** button to insert a new row. <New Task> appears as the task name.

b. Enter the task name Reserve golf course, and then press Tab. Enter a duration of 1 hour, and then press Tab. Reserve golf course becomes the new Task 4.

c. With Reserve golf course (Task 4) still selected, press Insert. A blank row is added above the selected row to create a new task.

> **Troubleshooting**
> If your keyboard does not have an Insert key, repeat Step a.

SIDE NOTE

Task Changes

When you make changes to a task, Project 2013 will highlight the affected tasks in the Entry table with a gray background.

d. In the Task Name cell for the new Task 4, enter the task name Perform site inspections, and then press Tab. Enter a duration of 4 hours, and then press Tab.

e. Click in the Duration column of row 3, **Set tournament date and time**, and then change the duration from 1 day to **4 hours**.

f. Double-click **Solicit potential tournament sponsors** (Task 8). This will open the Task Information dialog box.

g. If necessary, click the **General** tab. In the upper right-hand corner of the General tab, change the **Duration** from 1 week to **3 days**.

SIDE NOTE

Task Note

Double-click the **Note** icon or hover over the Note icon in the Indicators column to display the note.

h. Click the **Notes** tab. Add the note Contact local sporting goods stores for a list of potential sponsors.

Figure 27   Task Information dialog box Notes tab

i. Click **OK**. Notice the Note indicator in the Indicators column, and then click **Save**.

Task Note indicator

Figure 28 Note indicator in the Entry table

Deleting Project Tasks in the Entry Table

As a project planner, you may decide a project task is no longer needed. As well as inserting tasks, Project 2013 allows for tasks to be deleted. Deleting a task removes an entire task row and moves any subsequent tasks up a row. As with inserting tasks, there are several ways to delete tasks in Project 2013 such as using the Ribbon, the shortcut menu, or the keyboard.

Since the project team for this charity golf tournament is already in place, you will delete this task.

PM1.08 **To Delete a Task**

a. Right-click the row selector for **Determine project team** (Task 2).

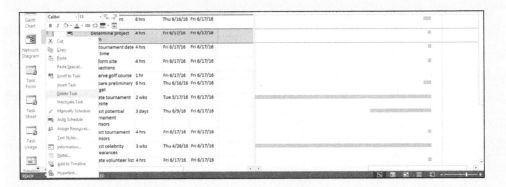

Figure 29 Task shortcut menu

b. Click **Delete Task** from the shortcut menu. Determine project team (Task 2) is deleted.

c. Click the row selector for **Create volunteer list** (Task 10). With the task selected, press Delete. Task 10 is now deleted.

d. On the Quick Access Toolbar click **Undo** ⟲ to undo the deletion of Task 10.

e. Click **Save** 🖫.

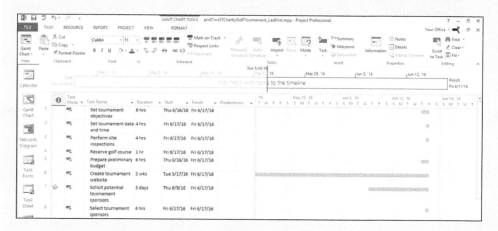

Figure 30 Entry table with project task deleted

Moving, Cutting, Copying, and Pasting Project Tasks in the Entry Table

Project planners may decide to reorder tasks or even copy tasks. Moving tasks will simply reorder tasks within the Entry table. If a task is cut, the task will be temporarily deleted and placed on the Project 2013 clipboard. If a task is copied, the task stays in its current location but is also placed on the clipboard to be pasted in another location in the Entry table. Any tasks on the clipboard can be pasted within the Entry table of the project.

After reviewing the project tasks, you have decided it is important to prepare your budget before you perform site inspections. Therefore, you will move Task 5.

PM1.09 To Move a Task

a. Click the row selector for **Prepare preliminary budget** (Task 5) to select the task.

b. When you see the 4-arrow pointer, press and hold the mouse button. Drag the row selector above **Perform site inspections** (Task 3). As you drag Task 5, a dark gray horizontal bar will indicate the position of the task if you were to let go of your mouse.

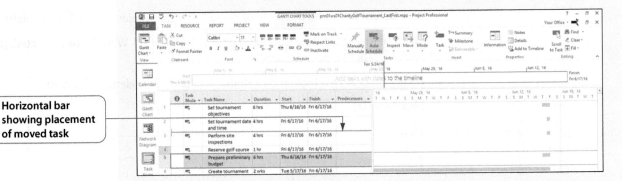

Figure 31 Moving a task in the Entry table

c. Release the mouse button. The **Prepare preliminary budget** task now becomes Task 3.

> **Troubleshooting**
> If you are having difficulty moving a task, be sure you first click the row selector of a task. Then click the task row selector again and drag the task to the desired location.

d. Right-click the row selector for **Set tournament objectives** (Task 1). Click **Copy** from the shortcut menu. Click in row 12, the first blank row, and then click **Paste** from the Clipboard group of the TASK tab. This creates a copy of the task.

e. Delete the copied task, and then click **Save**.

> **Troubleshooting**
> If you press Delete on the Task Name cell of a task row, Project 2013 will prompt you to 1) Delete the task name or 2) Delete the task. To avoid this prompt, select the task row selector, and then press Delete.

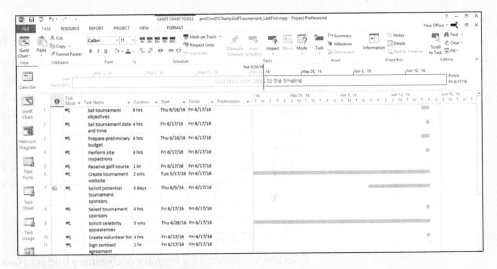

Figure 32 Entry table with task moved

Modifying Project Tasks in Other Project Views

The Project 2013 software has several views from which to edit or view your project tasks. You can switch from one view to the other using the View Bar, which appears at the left-hand side of the project window. **Gantt Chart view** displays tasks, task durations, and task dependencies in a Gantt chart with horizontal bars and is the default view in Project 2013. The length of the task bars in the Gantt chart relates to the task detail such as duration and the zoom of the timescale at the top of the Gantt chart.

Calendar view displays tasks as bars on a calendar in a monthly format. Calendar view may be used to see upcoming weekly or monthly tasks. Managers may also choose to print from Calendar view as it gives an overview of the week or month ahead.

Patti Rochelle, the tournament-planning manager, has asked you to add additional tasks to the charity golf tournament project plan. You decide to make these additions in the Calendar and Network Diagram views.

PM1.10 To Add and Modify Tasks in Calendar View

a. Click **Create volunteer list** (Task 10), and then click the **TASK** tab if necessary.

b. In the View group on the TASK tab, click the **Gantt Chart** arrow and click **Calendar** to switch to Calendar view.

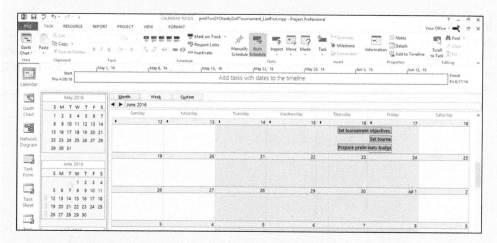

Figure 33 Calendar view

c. In Calendar view, click **Week** to change the calendar to Week view format.

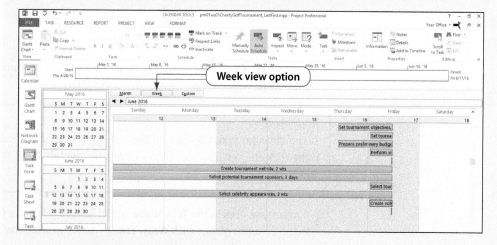

Figure 34 Week view option of Calendar view

d. With Calendar view in the Week format and Task 10 still selected, if necessary, click the **TASK** tab. In the Insert group, click the **Task** button to add a new blank task.

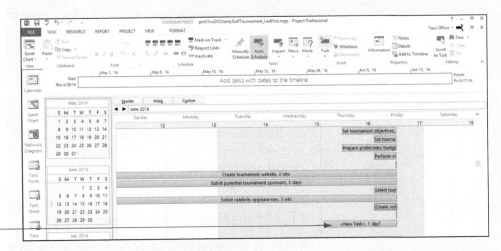

New task added

Figure 35 New task added in Calendar view

e. Double-click **<New Task> 1 day?** on the Calendar to open the Task Information dialog box.

f. On the General tab of the Task Information dialog box, add the task name **Begin online registrations**, and then press `Tab`. Enter a Duration of **0d**, and then click **OK**. Confirm the new task, Begin online registrations, has been added to the Calendar task list.

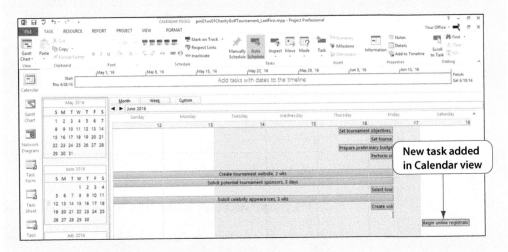

New task added
in Calendar view

Figure 36 Calendar view with new task added

g. Click **Gantt Chart** from the View Bar on the left-hand side of the Project 2013 window to view the new task in the Gantt chart.

> **Troubleshooting**
>
> If the View Bar is not visible on the left-hand side of the Project 2013 window, right-click the vertical text GANTT CHART on the left-hand side of the Project 2013 window and click View Bar.

h. If necessary, click in the Task Name cell of Task 10. Click the **GANTT CHART TOOLS** tab. In the Columns group, click **Wrap Text** twice to wrap the text of the new task.

i. Click the **Begin online registrations** (Task 10) row selector, and then move the task after **Create tournament website** (Task 6). Begin online registrations is now Task 7. Click **Save** ⊟.

> **Troubleshooting**
> If you add a new task and the Task Name is not word wrapping, click in the Task Name cell of the new task row and then click the GANTT CHART TOOLS tab. In the Columns group, click the Wrap Text button twice.

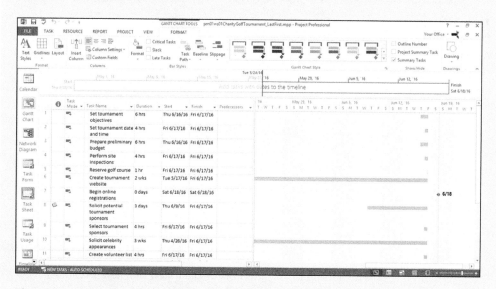

Figure 37   Gantt Chart view with new task added and moved

Not only can tasks be added in Gantt Chart view and Calendar view, they can also be added and modified in Network Diagram view. **Network Diagram view** also displays tasks and task dependencies. However, this view provides more information by displaying each task in a detailed box and clearly representing task dependencies with link lines. The **critical path** consists of tasks (or a single task) that determines the project's Finish date (or Start date); tasks on the critical path are considered critical tasks. The main purpose of the Network Diagram is to assist project managers in viewing the critical path.

Critical tasks are displayed in light red on the network diagram. A **critical task** must be completed on time in order to meet the project's finish date (or start date). A task becomes critical based on the task dependencies, task durations, and task resource assignments. Project managers must monitor critical tasks to be sure they are being completed on time in order to successfully meet the project schedule. You decide to switch to this view and add another project task.

PM1.11   To Add and Modify Tasks in Network Diagram View

a.   Click **Network Diagram** ▦ on the View Bar to switch to Network Diagram view.

b.   Scroll down the Network Diagram as necessary until you see **Begin online registrations** (ID: 7). Note the shape of this task is different from the other tasks with a rectangle shape because Task 7 is a milestone task.

SIDE NOTE

Identifying a Critical Task

Task 10 is a critical task because at this point in the planning process, Task 10 has the longest duration.

SIDE NOTE

Tasks in Network Diagram View

A selected task in the Network Diagram will appear with a black background and white text.

c. Scroll down again until you see **Solicit celebrity appearances** (Task 10). Note this task appears in red because it is a critical task.

d. While still in Network Diagram view scroll up, and then click **Create tournament website** (Task 6) to select the task.

e. Click the **TASK** tab, and then in the Insert group, click **Task** to add a new blank task in Network Diagram view. The new blank task becomes Task 6 with Task 7, Create tournament website, still selected.

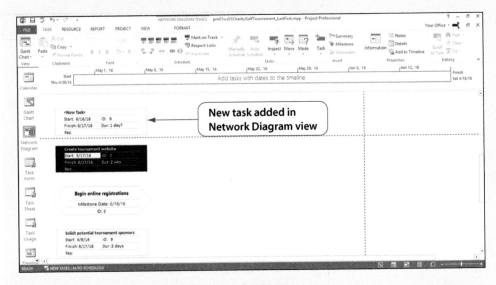

Figure 38   Network Diagram view with new task added

f. Double-click the **<New Task>** rectangle to open the Task Information dialog box. On the General tab of the Task Information dialog box, add the task name Design tournament logo, and then press [Tab].

g. Enter a Duration of 1d, and then click **OK**. The new task has the task name Design tournament logo with a duration of one day.

h. With **Design tournament logo** (Task 6) still selected, click one time in the **Dur:** box, type 2d, and then press [Enter] to change the duration of the task from 1 day to 2 days.

SIDE NOTE

Adding a New Task in the Network Diagram

You can also add a task in Network Diagram view by clicking in a blank area of the Network Diagram and dragging to draw a small rectangle.

> **Troubleshooting**
>
> If the Task 6 Task Information dialog box opened when attempting to adjust the duration, you double-clicked the task. Close the Task Information dialog box and click once to select Task 6.

Figure 39   New task added in Network Diagram

i. Select **Reserve golf course** (Task 5). Change the duration of Task 5 to 0d to make this task a milestone and change the shape of the task in Network Diagram view. With the milestone task still selected, click **Add to Timeline** in the Properties group on the TASK tab.

> **Troubleshooting**
>
> If the Timeline is not showing below the Ribbon, select the View tab, and then click the Timeline check box in the Split View group.

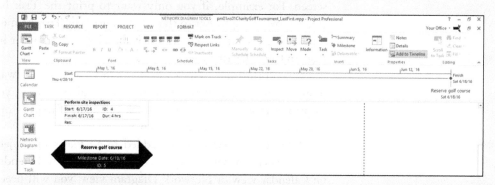

Figure 40 Timeline with Milestone added

j. Click **Gantt Chart** on the View Bar to return to Gantt Chart view. Note the new tasks, the change in durations, and milestone pinned to the Timeline. Click **Save** ⊞.

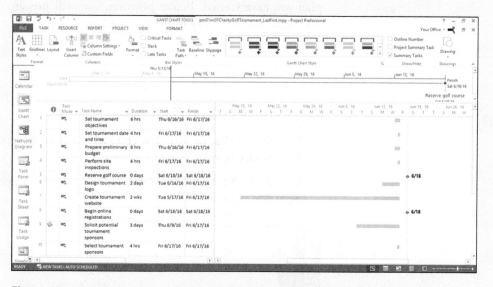

Figure 41 Gantt Chart view of the project plan with task additions and changes

---

CONSIDER THIS | **How can you motivate team members?**

Have you ever been a member of a team? How did your coach motivate you? Did your coach recognize team successes as they occurred? Project successes can be recognized by milestones. Therefore, milestones can help motivate the project team by recognizing project accomplishments.

Prepare Project for Printing Project Views

Various views can be printed in Project 2013. Prior to printing, it is important to set up the project view to the appropriate zoom, include any header or footer information, and be sure all printing options are set the way you desire. Printing options are found on the

FILE tab in Backstage view. **Backstage view** is where you manage your project file and perform tasks such as saving, printing, and setting project options. In Backstage view, you can preview each page layout before printing. You can also view the status of your project and make related project changes in Backstage view. Backstage view displays in full screen to allow for more window space to work with relevant features.

When printing in Gantt Chart view, the printout will appear as it looks on your screen. For example, if you only want to print the Task Name column and the Gantt chart, move the split bar to the right edge of the Task Name column with a left click and drag before printing. The default is for a legend to appear in the bottom portion of each page in Gantt Chart view.

When printing in Network Diagram view, you may want to zoom in or out to view more or fewer tasks. When printing from Calendar view, you should decide if you want to print a month calendar or a week calendar. If neither option fit your needs, you can customize a Calendar Print option.

A header or footer can be added to all views in Project 2013. However, adding a header in Gantt Chart view does not add a header to Calendar view. If you desire a header on Calendar view or Network Diagram view, you will need to add one in each view by clicking on the Page Setup link in the Backstage Print option.

Preparing to Print in Gantt Chart View

You want to print the Gantt chart to show the team the charity golf tournament project plan you have started. Before printing, you will prepare your project views by adding your name to the header in the Gantt Chart views.

PM1.12 **To Print in Gantt Chart View**

a. Drag the **split bar** between the Entry table and the Gantt chart to the right edge of the Finish date column in Gantt Chart view.

b. Click the **FILE** tab, and click **Print**. Your project will appear in the preview pane on the right side of the screen.

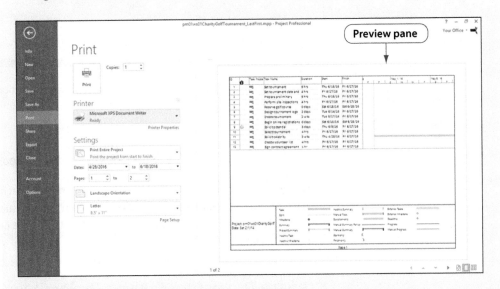

Figure 42   Gantt Chart in preview pane

Troubleshooting

The printer displayed in the Printer list is determined by your installation and may be different than the printer shown in Figure 42.

c. Click in the preview pane on the right-hand side of the Project 2013 window. The preview will zoom so you can see more detail.

d. Click the **Multiple Pages** [⊞] button in the lower, right-hand corner of the Preview pane to view both pages of Gantt Chart view.

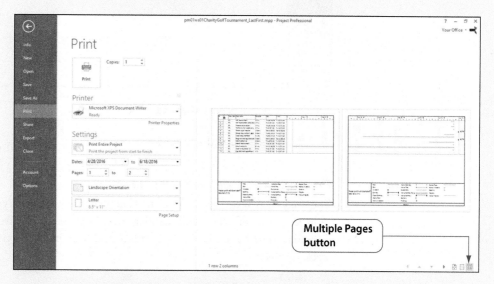

Figure 43   Preview Pane Navigation buttons

e. Click the **Page Setup** link. The Page Setup dialog box will open.

Figure 44   Page Setup dialog box

f. Click the **Header** tab. Click the **Right** tab, and then add your first and last name.

g. Click **OK**.

h. Click the **One Page** button [▯] in the lower, right-hand corner of the preview pane to view one page of the Gantt Chart along with your change to the header.

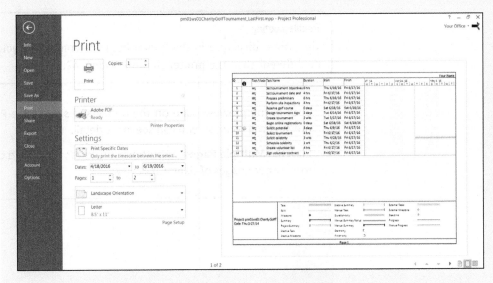

Figure 45 Preview pane with header added

i. Click **Back** , and then click **Save** .

Preparing to Print in Calendar View

You may also want to print from Calendar view to give your team members a visual representation of what will happen week to week. Before printing, you will prepare Calendar view by adding your name to the header and setting up the Calendar to print week by week.

PM1.13 To Print in Calendar View

a. Click **Calendar** on the View Bar.

b. Click the **FILE** tab, and then click **Print**.

c. Click the **Page Setup** link, and then click the **Header** tab. Click the **Right** tab, and then add your first and last name. Click **OK**.

d. To view the project tasks, click the list arrow for the starting date.

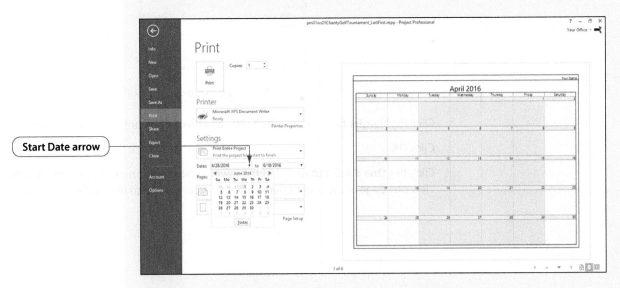

Start Date arrow

Figure 46 Setting start date preview in Calendar view preview pane

e.   Click **6/1/2016**.

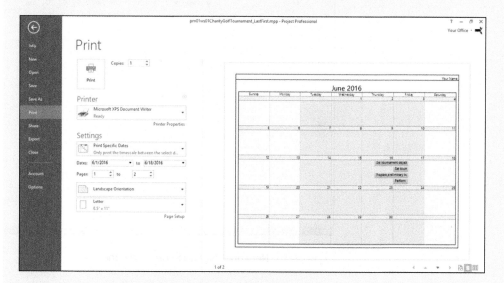

Figure 47   Calendar print preview setting

Troubleshooting

If you only see the month of April, use the view buttons in the lower right-hand corner of the preview window to scroll to the month of June in the preview pane.

---

f.   Click **Back** ⬅, and then click **Save** 🖫.

Preparing to Print in Network Diagram View

One of your team members has asked for a printout of the project's task to be in a graphical format, not in Calendar or Gantt Chart format. Therefore, you decide to print the project tasks in Network Diagram view.

PM1.14 To Print in Network Diagram View

a.   On the View Bar switch to **Network Diagram** ▦ view.

b.   Click the **FILE** tab, and then click **Print**.

c.   Click the **Page Setup** link, and then click the **Header** tab. Click the **Right** tab, and then add your first and last name. Click **OK**.

d.   Click the **Landscape Orientation** arrow, and then click **Portrait Orientation**.

e.   Use the **Page Navigation** buttons ◀ ▲ ▼ ▶ to scroll through the pages that will print. Note the shape of the milestone tasks in the Network Diagram.

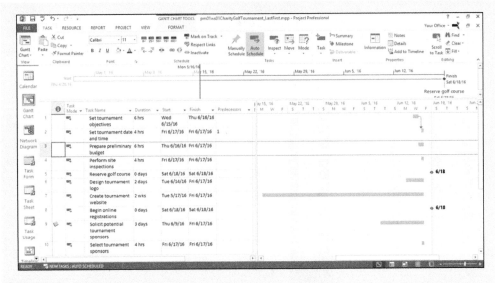

Figure 48 Network Diagram in preview pane

f. Click **Back** ⊝, and then click **Save** 🔲.

Create Task Dependencies

When creating a project schedule, if you do not define task dependencies, all tasks will start on the project Start date or finish on the project Finish date. However, in most projects, tasks may be dependent on other tasks. Therefore, Project 2013 allows project planners to create task dependencies.

Task dependencies create predecessor tasks and successor tasks. For example, you could not begin a task of "begin online registrations" without first completing the task of "set tournament date and time." In this case, "set tournament date and time" would be the predecessor task to "begin online registrations" (which then becomes the successor task). Remember, project managers often use the terms relationship, dependency, or link when referring to how the predecessor or successor tasks are connected.

> **CONSIDER THIS** | **Why create task dependencies?**
>
> Have you ever baked a cake? If so, then you know you need to purchase the ingredients before mixing them together; mix the ingredients together before pouring them into a pan; prepare the pan before pouring in the ingredients; heat the oven before putting the mixed ingredients into the oven to bake; etc. Baking a cake is a project during which tasks are completed in a certain order. This order is defined by task dependencies.

There are four types of task dependencies in Project 2013 as shown in Table 4:

Type	Detail	Example
Finish-to-Start (FS)	Default. Task 1 must finish before Task 2 can start.	You must finish selecting the tournament date (Task 1) before beginning online registration (Task 2).
Start-to-Start (SS)	Task 1 must start before Task 2 can start.	As soon as the tournament website goes live (Task 1) you can start accepting online registrations (Task 2).
Start-to-Finish (SF)	Task 1 must start before Task 2 can finish.	You must start working on the tournament website (Task 1) before you can finish promotional materials (Task 2).
Finish-to-Finish (FF)	Task 1 must finish before Task 2 can finish.	You must finish accepting online registrations (Task 1) before you finalize tournament supply list (Task 2).

Table 4 Task Dependencies

In Project 2013, task dependencies are recorded in the row for the second (successor) task. For example, if you are creating a dependency between "set the tournament date" (Task A) and "begin online registrations" (Task B), you record the dependency in the row for Task B.

Dependencies in the software are also often referred to as task relationships or task links. Project managers often use these terms interchangeably. If you are manually scheduling your project, you can still assign task dependencies. However, if manually scheduling, the task dependencies will not affect the project schedule.

There are several ways to create task dependencies to the default Finish-to-Start relationship:

- Select the tasks to be related in Gantt Chart, Network Diagram, or Calendar view, and then click the Link the Selected Tasks ⏣ button on the Task tab in the Schedule group as shown in Figure 49.

- Double-click a task in Gantt chart, Network Diagram, or Calendar view, and then click the Predecessors tab. Enter in the task row(s) of the predecessor task(s), and then click OK.

- In Gantt chart, Network Diagram, or Calendar view, select the predecessor task with a left-click and drag to the successor task. Release the mouse and the tasks become linked.

- In Gantt Chart view, click the successor task to select the task. In the Predecessors column, enter the task row(s) of the related task(s), and then press [Enter].

- Select the tasks to be related and press [CTRL] + [F2].

Link the selected tasks

Figure 49   Task tab Schedule group

Adding Task Dependencies

In order to create a more detailed project plan, you have been asked to create task dependencies for the tournament project tasks.

PM1.15 To Set Task Dependencies

a. Click **Gantt Chart** 🗓 on the View Bar. Move the **split bar** between the Gantt chart and the Entry table to the right edge of the Predecessors column by dragging the **split bar** to the right.

b. Select **Set tournament objectives** (Task 1) and **Set tournament date and time** (Task 2), and then click the **TASK** tab. In the Schedule group, click **Link the Selected Tasks** ⏣. Linking Tasks 1 and 2 created a Finish-to-Start relationship. Note the link line in the Gantt chart as well as the change to the Start date in Task 1. Also note a "1" was added to the Predecessors column in Row 2.

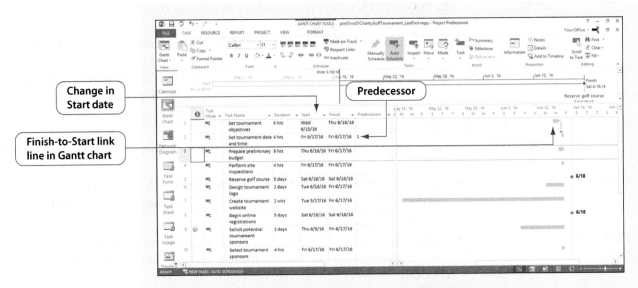

Change in Start date

Predecessor

Finish-to-Start link line in Gantt chart

Figure 50 Finish-to-Start relationship created in the Entry table

c. Click in the **Predecessors** column for **Prepare preliminary budget** (Task 3). Type a **2** and press Enter. Task 2 becomes a predecessor of Task 3.

d. In the Gantt chart on the right-hand side of your screen, click and hold the Prepare **preliminary budget** (Task 3) Gantt bar and then drag to the **Perform site inspections** (Task 4) Gantt bar.

SIDE NOTE

Linking Tasks

When linking tasks in the Gantt chart, you will see the 🔗 Link the Selected Tasks symbol as you drag from one task bar to the next.

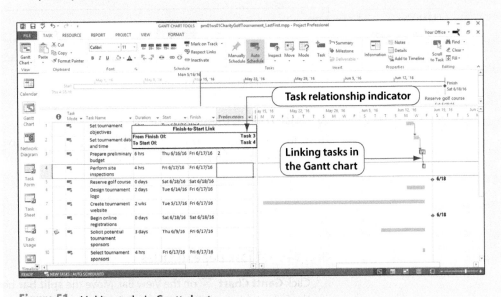

Task relationship indicator

Linking tasks in the Gantt chart

Figure 51 Linking tasks in Gantt chart

e. Release the mouse button to create a relationship between Tasks 3 and 4.

f. Double-click **Reserve golf course** (Task 5) to open the Task Information dialog box. Click the **Predecessors** tab. Click in the ID column of the first row of the Predecessors table. Enter a **4** in the ID column of the first row, and then press Tab to assign the predecessor of Task 4, **Perform site inspections**.

SIDE NOTE

Scrolling to Task

To view a task from the Entry table that is not visible in the Gantt chart, right-click the task and click Scroll to Task.

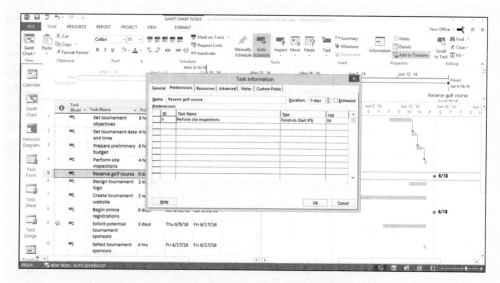

Figure 52 Assigning predecessors in the Task Information dialog box

g. Click **OK**, and then select Task 1, **Set tournament objectives**. On the View Bar, click **Network Diagram** 🔲. Click and hold **Set tournament objectives** (Task 1), and then drag to **Design tournament logo** (Task 6).

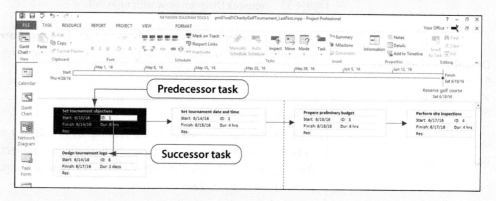

Figure 53 Linking tasks in Network Diagram view

h. Release the mouse button to create a Finish-to-Start relationship between Task 1 and Task 6.

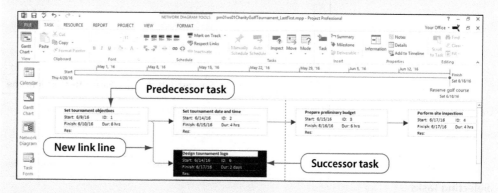

Figure 54 Linked tasks in Network Diagram view

> **Troubleshooting**
>
> If you do not see the tasks in Network Diagram view you desire, you may need to scroll to the left or right to view the tasks. You can also click the Zoom button from the Zoom group of the VIEW tab, and then select from the Zoom In or Zoom Out options.

i.   Click and hold **Prepare preliminary budget** (Task 3) and drag to **Design tournament logo** (Task 6). Tasks 3 and 6 now have a Finish-to-Start relationship.

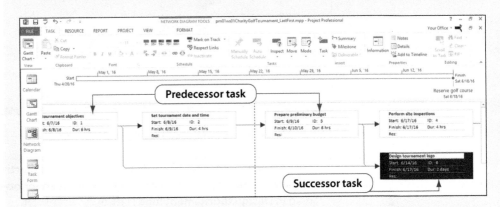

Figure 55   Network Diagram view with tasks linked

j.   Switch to **Calendar view** 📅. Click and hold **Design tournament logo** (Task 6), and drag to **Create tournament website** (Task 7). Release the mouse button to create a relationship between Tasks 6 and 7.

SIDE NOTE

Dragging to Link Tasks
If you selected Task 7 and dragged to Task 6, the relationship would have a different result than selecting Task 6 and dragging to Task 7.

> **Troubleshooting**
>
> If you do not see the tasks you are looking for in Calendar view, be sure your Calendar is showing the correct month in which your project tasks are scheduled. You may need to change the Calendar to Week view and expand the week view and scroll to the week of June 14, 2016.

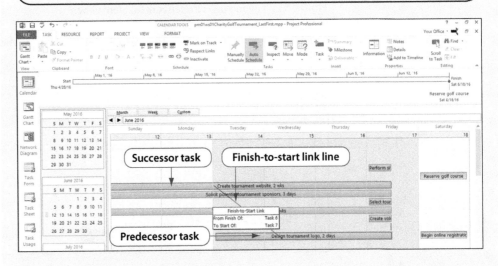

Figure 56   Linking tasks in Calendar view

SIDE NOTE

Selecting Tasks
When you select more than one row in an Entry table, the selected tasks will be shaded.

k.   Return to Gantt Chart 📊 view. Select **Tasks 7-13** by selecting the task row selectors. Press `Ctrl` + `F2`. All task relationships are now defined. Click **Save** 💾.

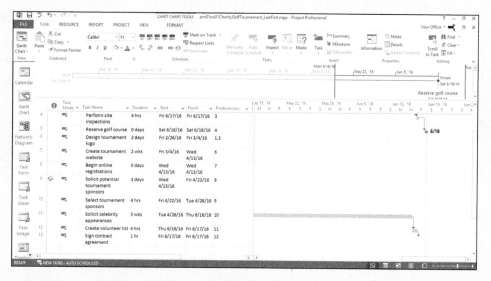

Figure 57 Gantt Chart view with task relationships defined

Modify Task Dependencies and Task Constraints

Although setting task relationships and task constraints is an important part of the planning process, it is equally important for project managers to evaluate the task relationships and constraints to be sure the results are logical. Therefore, Project 2013 allows project managers to modify, add, or delete task relationships and task constraints throughout the planning process. Task constraints can be modified by using the Task Information dialog box Advanced tab.

Task relationships can be added, deleted, or modified in the following ways:

- Using the Predecessors column of Gantt Chart view
- Using the Task Information dialog box Predecessors tab
- Double-clicking the link line in Gantt Chart and Network Diagram views and using the Task Dependency dialog box

On the charity golf tournament project plan, the task of Reserve golf course (Task 5) is scheduled to begin on the day of the tournament and Create volunteer list (Task 12) is scheduled to begin the day before the tournament. Knowing these tasks must occur before the dates Project 2013 is scheduling, you decide to make a modification to your project plan. Before you modify task relationships, it is important to understand how a task is being scheduled. For example, Reserve golf course (Task 5) is scheduled to happen the day of the event. There are two possible reasons for the scheduling of this task:

- The task has a constraint of As Late As Possible because the project is scheduled by Finish date
- Task 5 is not a predecessor to any other tasks in this project.

Although a project may be set to Auto Scheduled, ultimately the project manager of the project has control over the schedule of tasks. For example, a project manager can add, delete, or change task relationships and/or task constraints to adjust the project schedule.

Modifying Dependencies and Constraints

You realize the scheduling of these tasks does not work with your project plan, so you explore ways of adjusting how these tasks are scheduled.

To Modify Task Dependencies and Task Constraints

SIDE NOTE

Task Constraints

Changing the constraint from As Late As Possible to As Soon As Possible allows the task to begin once its predecessor tasks are complete.

a. Double-click **Reserve golf course** (Task 5), and then click the **Advanced** tab in the Task Information dialog box. Click the **Constraint type** arrow and change the task constraint to **As Soon As Possible**. Click **OK**. Note that the milestone date changed and moved on the Timeline.

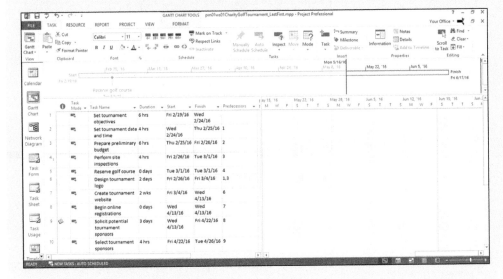

Figure 58 Modified task constraint

b. Select **Create volunteer list** (Task 12). If necessary, right-click the task and click **Scroll to Task** to view the task and its predecessor in the Gantt chart.

c. Press [Insert] to add a blank task row. Add the task name Schedule celebrity appearances, add a duration of **1w** and then press [Tab]. Press [Tab] two more times, and then enter 11 as the predecessor for the new Task 12.

d. In the Gantt chart, double-click the **link line** between Tasks 11 and 13 to open the Task Dependency dialog box. In the Task Dependency dialog box, click the **Type** arrow. Click **Start-to-Start**.

Figure 59 Task Dependency dialog box

e. Click **OK**.

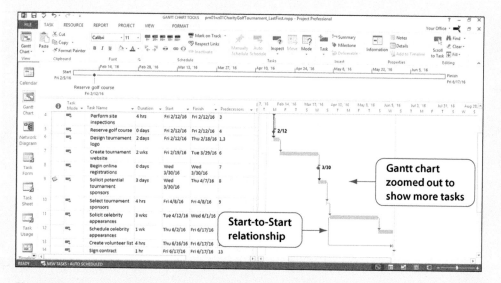

Figure 60   Start-to-Start relationship

f. Create volunteer list (Task 13) is still scheduled to start the day before the tournament. Therefore, double-click **Create volunteer list** (Task 13). Click the **Advanced** tab, and then change the Constraint type to **As Soon As Possible**. Click **OK.**

g. Select **Sign contract agreement** (Task 14). Press F2 on the keyboard to enter Edit mode. Click in front of the **c** on contract and add volunteer and press the space bar. Add an **s** to the end of agreement. Press Enter to accept the change.

h. Double click **Sign volunteer contract agreements** (Task 14) to open the Task Information dialog box. Click the **Advanced** tab. Enter a **Constraint date** of 6/1/16.

i. Click **OK**. Note the Constraint indicator in the Indicators column.

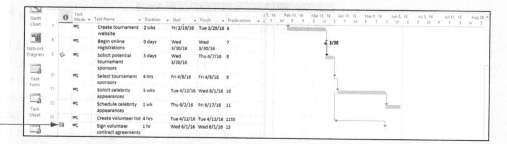

Figure 61   Constraint indicator

j. Select **Begin online registrations** (Task 8), and then in the Properties group on the TASK tab, click **Add to Timeline** . **Save** the project file.

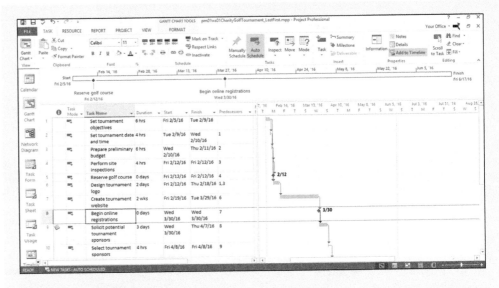

Figure 62 Gantt Chart view of project plan

If a project is scheduled by Start date, another way to modify task dependencies is to create lag time or lead time. **Lag time** moves a successor task forward in time so the Start date between the tasks become further apart. **Lead time** moves a successor task back in time so the two tasks overlap and the Start date between the tasks gets closer. Lead time is the opposite of lag time and is sometimes referred to as negative lag. Lag time will likely extend the length of the project.

REAL WORLD ADVICE | **Using Lag Time in a Project**

In projects, some tasks can be assigned to begin past the task's original assigned start date by adding a lag time. For example, a task "website goes live" may have a successor task of "analyze website traffic" with a start-to-start relationship. Although you can start analyzing website traffic at the start of the website going live, it makes sense to wait a week or two before you begin analyzing data. In this case, you would add lag time to the dependency. Adding lag time to tasks on the critical path will increase the overall project's duration. Lag time can be added by:

- Double-clicking the link line between tasks in the Gantt Chart or the Network Diagram.
- In the Task Dependency dialog box, entering a duration in number or percentage format.

Deleting Task Dependencies

After linking tasks and setting task dependencies, you may decide a dependency is no longer needed or was created in error. Project 2013 allows you to not only modify task dependencies but also delete task dependencies.

You realize the scheduling of these tasks does not work with your project plan, so you explore ways of adjusting how these tasks are scheduled.

To Delete a Task Dependency

a. Click in the Predecessors column for **Sign volunteer contract agreements** (Task 14).

b. In the Schedule group of the TASK tab, click **Unlink Tasks** 🔗. Note the task Start date did not change because a Constraint date has been set on the task.

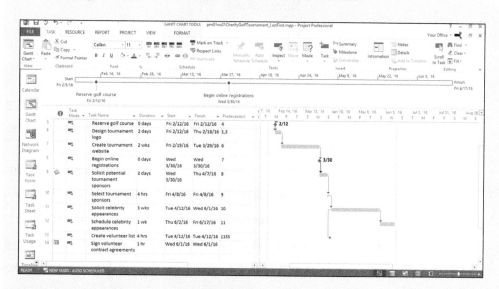

Figure 63   Gantt Chart view with unlinked task

c. **Save** and submit your project file as directed by your instructor.

Concept Check

1. Explain the following terms to someone new to the Project 2013 software:

   a. Predecessor task

   b. Successor task

   c. Constraint

   d. Milestone

2. What is the purpose of a Gantt chart?

3. Describe the components of the Project Information dialog box.

4. Why is it important for a project's base calendar to accurately reflect the available working time of a project?

5. Describe the difference between a Manually Scheduled and an Auto Scheduled project.

6. List the task durations and task abbreviations in Project.

7. How can a Note be applied to a task? When would a Note be applied to a task?

8. How do you add your name to the header of the Gantt chart?

9. Describe at least three ways you can add task dependencies.

10. Describe at least three ways you can change a task dependency between tasks.

Key Terms

Modify the Quick Access Toolbar and Collapse the Ribbon (p. 9)

Prepare a Project Schedule (p. 10)

Change the Project Information (p. 12)

Modify a Project Calendar (p. 12)

Change the Project Calendar Working Time (p. 13)

Add an Exception to the Project Calendar (p. 15)

Understand Manually Scheduled Versus Auto Scheduled Projects (p. 17)

Print in Calendar View (p. 34)

Print in Network Diagram View (p. 35)

Move a Task (p. 25)

Prepare Project for Printing Project Views (p. 31)

Add and Modify Tasks in Network Diagram View (p. 29)

Modify a Task List (p. 23)

Delete a Task (p. 24)

Enter Project Tasks (p. 21)

Modify Project Tasks in Project Views (p. 22)

Print in Gantt Chart View (p. 32)

Create Task Dependencies (p. 36)

Modify Task Dependencies and Task Constraints (p. 42)

Delete a Task Dependency (p. 45)

Add and Modify Tasks in Calendar View (p. 27)

Set a Project to Auto Scheduled (p. 19)

Identify Project Tasks (p. 19)

Set Task Dependencies (p. 37)

Modify Task Dependencies and Task Constraints (p. 41)

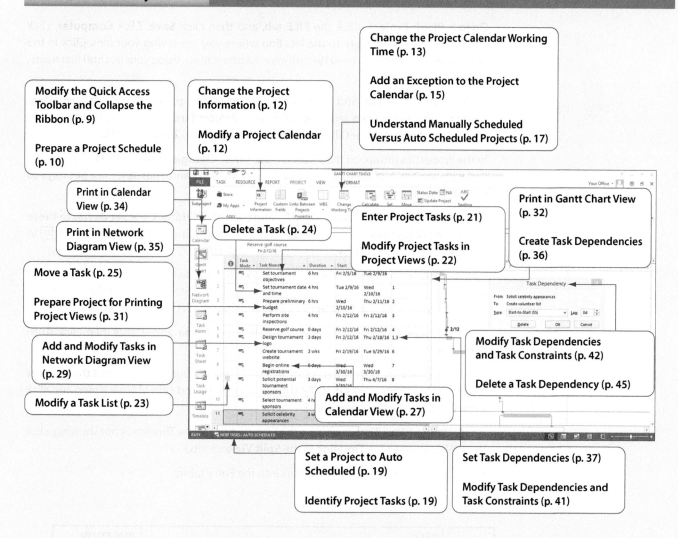

Figure 64 Project 2013 Charity Golf Tournament Plan

Practice

Student data file needed:
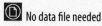 No data file needed

You will save your file as:
pm01ws01BloodDrive_LastFirst.mpp

Organizing a Blood Drive at Your Community College

You have been asked by the student senate to be the project lead of a blood drive at your school to promote a cause that saves millions of lives each year. To demonstrate your project management skills, you decide to use Project 2013 to set up the plan for the blood drive. You have been given the date of October 14, 2016 as the date the event will take place.

Your college is closed on October 7, 2016, and you are available to work on this project Wednesday through Friday, 8:00 A.M. to 12:00 P.M.

a. Open a **Blank Project**. Click the **FILE** tab, and then click **Save**. Click **Computer**, click **Browse**, and then navigate to the location where you are saving your files. Click in the **File name** box, type pm01ws01BloodDrive_LastFirst.mpp, using your last and first name, and then click **Save**.

b. Click the **PROJECT** tab, and then in the Properties group, click **Project Information.** Select the **Schedule from** arrow and change to **Project Finish Date** to set the project to schedule by finish date. Set the Finish date to **October 14, 2016**. Click **OK**.

c. In the Properties group, on the PROJECT tab, select **Change Working Time** 📅. Click the **Work Weeks** tab, and then click **Details**. Select **Monday** and **Tuesday**. Click **Set days to nonworking time**.

d. Click **Wednesday**, press and hold ⎡Shift⎤, and then click **Friday**. Click **Set day(s) to these specific working times**. Select row **2** in the specific working times grid. Press ⎡Delete⎤ to clear the 1:00 P.M. to 5:00 P.M. working times. Click **OK**.

e. Click the **Exceptions tab** in the Change Working Time dialog box. Enter the exception name College closed, and then press ⎡Tab⎤. Click in the Start column in Row 1. Change the start date in row 1 to **October 7, 2016**, and then press ⎡Tab⎤. Click **OK**.

f. Click the **TASK** tab. In the Tasks group select the **Mode** arrow, and then click **Auto Schedule**.

g. Be sure the View Bar is showing on the left-hand side of your screen. (Hint: If the View Bar is not showing, right-click **GANTT CHART** on the left-hand side of your screen and click **View Bar** from the shortcut menu.)

h. If necessary, add the Timeline below the Ribbon. (Hint: If the Timeline is not showing, click the **VIEW** tab and click **Timeline** in the **Split View** group.)

i. Enter the following tasks and durations into the Entry table:

	TASK	DURATION
1	Select blood drive campus location	4 hours
2	Set blood drive goal	1 hour
3	Form a recruitment team	2 days
4	Divide team roles and duties	2 hours
5	Plan promotional strategies	4 hours
6	Publicize the blood drive	1 day
7	Schedule appointments	2 weeks
8	Check site arrangements	4 hours
9	Get visitor parking passes	2 hours
10	Email appointment reminder messages	4 hours
11	Post directional arrows and posters around campus	1 hour

j. Select **Publicize the blood drive** (Task 6). Press ⎡Insert⎤ to add a blank task. With the new blank task selected, add the task name Create promotional materials. Assign this task a duration of **5 hours**.

k. Select the row selector of **Get visitor parking passes** (Task 10). While holding the mouse, drag Task 10 after E-mail appointment reminder messages (Task 11). Release the mouse. Get visitor parking passes is now moved to become Task 11.

l. Click **Publicize the blood drive** (Task 7). Click the **TASK** tab, and then in the **Insert** group click **Task** to add a new task. Enter the task name Contact local businesses and give the task a duration of 6 hours. Task 7 is now Contact local businesses.

m. Double-click **Contact local businesses** (Task 7) to open the **Task Information dialog box**. Click the **Notes** tab. Add the task note Contact the webmaster to place blood drive info on college website. Click **OK**.

n. Click the **FILE** tab, and then click **Print**. Click the **Page Setup** link, and then click the **Header** tab. Click the **Right** tab, and then add your first and last name in the right tab **Header**. Click **OK**.

o. Exit Backstage view and return to Gantt Chart view. Click **Network Diagram** 📧 on the View Bar. Select **Post directional arrows and posters around campus** (Task 13). Click the **TASK** tab, and then in the **Insert** group, click **Task** 📇 to add a new task in Network Diagram view.

p. Double-click the new task, and then add the task name Blood drive begins and set the duration to 0 days to make this task a milestone. Click **OK**. Note the shape of the Milestone task in the Network Diagram view.

q. With **Blood drive begins** (Task 13) selected, click **Add to Timeline** in the Properties group of the TASK tab. The milestone is now added to the Timeline.

r. Click **Gantt Chart** on the View Bar to switch to Gantt Chart view.

s. Move Task 13, Blood drive begins, after **Post directional arrows and posters around campus** (Task 14) to make it the final project task.

t. Select **Tasks 1-14**. Click Ctrl + F2 to link all the tasks.

u. Select **Schedule appointments** (Task 9) and change the duration from 2 weeks to 20 hours.

v. Open the Task Information dialog box for **Email appointment reminder messages** (Task 11), and then click the **Advanced** tab. Set a **Constraint date** to **October 13, 2016**.

w. Change the relationship to a Start-to-Start relationship between Schedule appointments (Task 9) and Check site arrangements (Task 10).

x. Change the Predecessor of **Get visitor parking passes** (Task 12) to 9SS. Double-click Task 12 and then click the **Advanced** tab. Change the Constraint type to **As Soon As Possible**.

y. Save your **pm01ws01BloodDrive_LastFirst** project, and then close the project file. Submit your file as directed by your instructor.

Problem Solve

Student data file needed:
🔲 No data file needed

You will save your file as:
🔲 pm01ws01JobSearchPortfolio_LastFirst.mpp

Planning Your Job Search Portfolio

You will be graduating in May 2016 from your program of study at your local community college. You decide it is time to start preparing for your job search portfolio. You begin brainstorming a list of tasks, and you realize there are many tasks that need to be completed. To be sure you don't miss an important step, you decide to use Project 2013 to help you organize and keep track of your task list.

a. Open a blank Project 2013 file and save it as pm01ws01JobSearchPortfolio_LastFirst.mpp in the location where you store your files.

b. Since you are just starting your portfolio, you will leave the default schedule of **Project Start Date**. Set the Start date to **February 1, 2016**. Set the current date **January 25, 2016**.

c. Due to other school obligations, you can only dedicate 10 hours a week to work on your portfolio. To stay on task, you will work 2 hours per day Monday through Friday. You have afternoon classes so you will set **8:00 A.M.** to **10:00 A.M.** as working time. The remainder of the days and times will be set to nonworking time.

d. Add the Exception Spring Break to make **March 23-25, 2016** nonworking days.

e. Set the project to **Auto Scheduled** so the task dates are calculated by Project 2013.

f. Enter in the following tasks:

	TASK	DURATION
1	Purchase portfolio supplies	2 h
2	Get an unofficial transcript	4 h
3	Identify references	1 w
4	Write resume	6 h
5	Create a resume in PDF format	2 h
6	Write a cover letter	3 h
7	Conduct online job search	5 d
8	Gather work examples for portfolio	10 h
9	Conduct a mock interview	3 h
10	Send resumes to potential employers	2 h
11	Compile portfolio	4 h

g. Select **Create a resume in PDF format** (Task 5). Add a note to Task 5 Use a PDF resume for online applications.

h. With Task 5 still selected, in a Project 2013 view of your choice, add a new task Edit resume with a duration of 2 hours. The Edit resume task becomes Task 5.

i. Add your first and last name as a header on the right tab of Gantt Chart, Network Diagram, and Calendar views. Change the Calendar view to **Week**. Return to Gantt Chart view.

j. Move **Write a cover letter** (Task 7) after **Conduct online job search** (Task 8). The Write a cover letter task becomes Task 8.

k. Add the task note Contact Career Resource Center. to **Gather work examples for portfolio** (Task 9). Click **OK**.

l. Change the duration of **Identify references** (Task 3) to **8 hours**.

m. In Gantt Chart view, move the split bar to the right edge of the Predecessors column. Link Tasks 1–12 in the order they appear in the Entry table.

n. If the **Timeline** is showing, remove it from Gantt Chart view.

o. Hide the **View Bar**.

p. Hide the **Task Mode** column (Hint: Right-click the Task Mode column).

q. Save your **pm01ws01JobSearchPortfolio_LastFirst.mmp** project, and then close the project file.

r. Submit your file as directed by your instructor.

Perform 1: Perform in Your Life

Student data file needed:

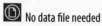 No data file needed

You will save your file as:

pm01ws01BusinessPlan_LastFirst.mpp

Preparing a Business Plan

You have decided to start a virtual assistant business in which you work from your home offering office-related assistance and software solutions to local businesses. In order to secure funding for your business, you must prepare a detailed business plan. You decide to use Project 2013 to help organize the details of preparing your business plan. Your goal is to have the business plan completed by July 1, 2016.

Based on your knowledge of preparing a Project 2013 file, you will:

a. Determine if you will set your project to schedule by Start date or by Finish date. As directed by your instructor, explain why you chose Start date or Finish date.

b. Adjust the Standard calendar for a work week maximum of 20 hours of working time. Any combination of days and hours are acceptable. Add a minimum of one exception to the calendar.

c. As directed by your instructor, explain the adjustments made to the calendar and detail any exceptions to the calendar.

d. Determine if you want to schedule your project by auto scheduled or manually scheduled. As directed by your instructor, explain how you set Project 2013 to schedule your project and why you chose that method.

e. Research preparing a business plan. There is more than one way to prepare a business plan. (Hint: Open Excel 2013 and in the Search box, type business plan.) You will use Project 2013 to enter a list of tasks you would need to complete to prepare your Virtual Assistant business plan. You must list a minimum of **10** key tasks to preparing a business plan. For example, Step 1 (Task 1) may be "Create a mission statement."

f. After identifying a minimum of 10 key steps to preparing a business plan, determine task durations based on your research and/or knowledge of preparing a business plan. Take into consideration your time available to work on the tasks as well.

g. Create appropriate task relationships (dependencies) for the project tasks. Assign a relationship other than Finish-to-Start to at least one task. As directed by your instructor, explain why you selected the task relationships for the project tasks.

h. Add at least one task constraint. As directed by your instructor, explain why you added the constraint and how it affects the project plan.

i. Add your first and last name as a header in Gantt Chart, Network Diagram, and Calendar views. Save your project as **pm01ws01BusinessPlan_LastFirst.mpp** in the location where you store your files.

j. Close your project. Submit your **pm01ws01BusinessPlan_LastFirst.mpp** file as directed by your instructor.

WORKSHOP 2 | CREATING A DETAILED PROJECT PLAN

Prepare Case

Painted Paradise Golf Resort – First Annual Charity Golf Tournament

© itsallgood/Fotolia

The Painted Paradise Golf Resort will be holding its first annual charity golf tournament to raise money for the purchase of textbooks to be donated to the elementary schools in Santa Fe, New Mexico. Patti Rochelle, the project manager of this event, has assigned you to start an initial list of project tasks using Microsoft Project 2013 to organize this event. She has looked over your list of tasks and made a few adjustments. Now Patti is asking you to develop a more detailed project plan by creating a Work Breakdown Structure for this project and assigning resources to individual tasks.

REAL WORLD SUCCESS

"Microsoft Office Project is a great way to plan any large project. I have used it to help plan my new business. I thought I was well prepared to start my new business, but little did I know how unprepared I was. As I started listing the steps I would need, I thought of one I forgot. I started out with 25 items, but when I was done, I had 81. Without Project, I would not be as prepared as I am today to become the entrepreneur I've always wanted to be."

—Angela, current student and entrepreneur

Student data files needed for this workshop:

 pm01ws02CharityGolfTournament.mmp

 pm01ws02CharityGolfTournamentTasks.xlsx

You will save your files as:

 pm01ws02CharityGolfTournament_LastFirst.mpp

pm01ws02CharityGolfTournament_LastFirst.docx

pm01ws02CharityGolfTournament_LastFirst.xlsx

 pm01ws02CharityGolfTournamentCalendar_LastFirst.docx

pm01ws02CharityGolfTournamentExport_LastFirst.xlsx

pm01ws02SimpleProjectPlan_LastFirst.mpp

pm01ws02EventTemplate_LastFirst.mpt

pm01ws02EventTemplate_LastFirst.mpp

Detailing a Project Plan

Project managers may choose to use Microsoft Project 2013 to assist them in planning and achieving project success. Project 2013 can provide project managers with an orderly way of creating a project schedule. To determine a project's schedule, project managers must adjust a project's calendar to reflect available working time, determine a project's scheduling method of automatic or manual, identify the project's tasks, define task relationships, and set task resources. Once this has been accomplished, project managers will have an idea of when the project should start or when the project should finish. However, project managers should not rely on the software to make all the scheduling decisions for a project. After all, Project 2013 is an application used to assist project managers in meeting the project goal, but it should not be the decision-making authority on the project plan.

Identify the Critical Path

Project managers create a project plan by setting task dependencies (relationships). By setting task dependencies, Project 2013 will create the critical path. The critical path consists of tasks that must be completed on time in order for a project to stay on track and come to a successful completion.

Creating task dependencies changes the start and finish dates of tasks. Creating task dependencies also creates the project's critical path. The critical path consists of tasks (or a single task) that determine the project's finish date (or start date). It is a list of tasks that must be completed on time for the project to meet the project timeline. Tasks on the critical path are critical tasks. Critical tasks do not have slack. **Slack** is the time a task can be delayed from its scheduled start date without delaying the project.

The best way to view the critical path is in Network Diagram view. In Network Diagram view, the critical path is represented by red task boxes and red link lines. This view can help project managers analyze the critical path and critical tasks and make informed project decisions. The critical path is not visible in Calendar view. By default, it is also not displayed in Gantt Chart view but you can add it to Gantt Chart view if desired.

Identifying the Critical Path

You want to view your project's critical path so you are aware of which tasks are critical tasks and therefore must be completed on time. You will view the project's critical path in Network Diagram and Gantt Chart views.

PM2.00 To View the Critical Path

PM2.00

a. Open Microsoft Project 2013. Navigate to the location of your student data files and browse for **pm01ws02CharityGolfTournament.mpp**, and then click **Open**.

b. Click the **FILE** tab, and then click **Save As**. Click **Computer**, and then if necessary click **Browse** and navigate to the location where you are storing your files. Click in the File name box and type pm01ws02CharityGolfTournament_LastFirst using your last and first name. Click **Save** 🖫.

c. Click **Network Diagram** 🖼 view from the View Bar. Scroll through Network Diagram view to view the project's tasks. The tasks in red are critical tasks. The tasks that do not appear in red are considered non-critical tasks.

Troubleshooting

If the View Bar is not visible on the left-hand side of the Project window as shown in Figure 1, right-click the vertical text GANTT CHART on the left-hand side of the Project window and click View Bar.

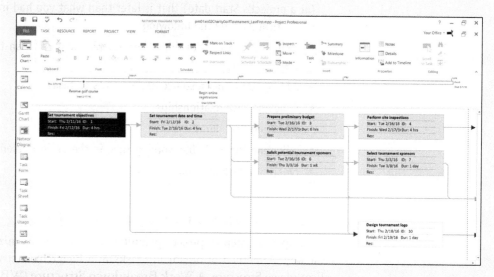

Figure 1   Critical Path in Network Diagram view

d. Return to **Gantt Chart** view, and then click the **GANTT CHART TOOLS FORMAT** tab.

e. In the Bar Styles group, click the **Critical Tasks** check box to add the Critical path to Gantt Chart view. Notice the critical path on the Gantt chart.

Critical Tasks check box

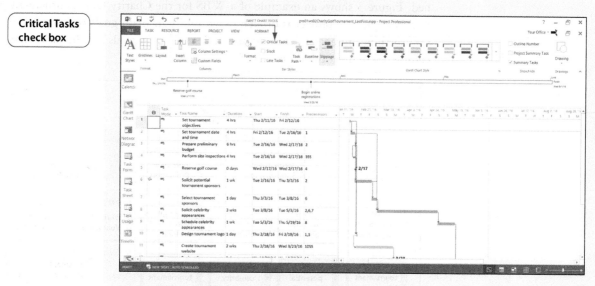

Figure 2   Gantt Chart view with critical path

f. Click the **Critical Tasks** check box again to remove the critical path from the Gantt chart.

Entering tasks, defining task relationships, assigning project resources, and adjusting the project calendar all affect how Project determines the critical path. However, project managers still have control over the project's critical path and should be the final decision makers of the project plan. If Project predicts a project's finish date (or a project's Start date) that is later than what you had in mind, you can shorten the critical path by the following:

- changing task relationships (for example, change finish-to-start relationship to a start-to-start)
- adding additional resource assignments to tasks
- removing task relationships
- adjusting task durations
- adjusting the available working time in the project calendar
- creating a task calendar

Create a Work Breakdown Structure

An important step to project planning success is to organize the project tasks in a logical way. A method of organizing tasks in a hierarchical structure is by creating a Work Breakdown Structure. A **Work Breakdown Structure (WBS)** creates a project plan structure in which project tasks are identified, task relationships are defined, and task resources are assigned. When creating a WBS, a project manager will define the main goals of the scope of a project and then identify the tasks that must go into completing these goals.

A WBS is often created in a top-down structure, similar to a detailed outline, where the main goals are defined and then supporting tasks to complete these goals are identified. Figure 3 shows an example of a WBS for the Charity Golf Tournament project. In this example, the project is broken down into four main goals of tournament initiation, sponsorship, promotion, and events. Under the main goals are the tasks that need to be completed to meet the project goal.

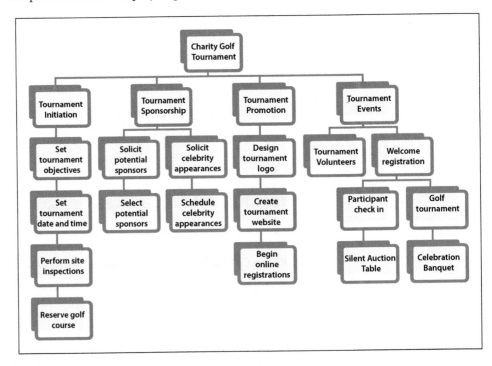

Figure 3 WBS example

Projects may also be broken into phases in which each phase is a main heading or goal in a WBS, and the steps to complete each phase are the individual tasks. If you recall, the phases of the project management planning process are initiation, planning, executing, monitoring, and closing. It is common for project managers to plan a project by these phases. Some managers, however, may choose phases that are more specific to their project plan.

Creating a Work Breakdown Structure

In order to create a Work Breakdown Structure in Project 2013, you must identify the main project goals or phases of the project. The main goals are like main headings in an outline. These main headings or goals are called summary tasks in the Project software. **Summary tasks** are tasks listed in bold in the Entry table and are groups of tasks that logically belong together. In Figure 3 above, an example of a summary task is Tournament Promotion. Summary tasks are not tasks that are to be completed; rather they are headings for grouped tasks. Related tasks that further define the summary tasks are called **subtasks**.

To create summary tasks, you can indent and outdent tasks or use the Summary button on the Insert group of the Task tab. **Indenting** a task moves a task to the right in the Entry table and makes it a lower level task in a WBS, such as a task that needs to be completed to achieve the main goal. **Outdenting** a task moves a task to the left in the Entry table and makes it a higher level in a WBS, such as a main goal. As shown in Figure 4, indenting and outdenting tasks can be done from the Schedule group of the Task tab.

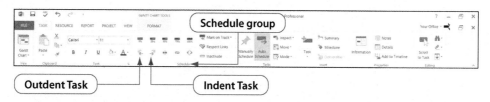

Figure 4   Task tab Schedule group

You can add new tasks to create summary tasks as well. Once a new task is added and given a main goal title, the related tasks would be indented to make the newly added task the summary task. Due to the flexibility of Project 2013, you can change the level of any task by outdenting or indenting the task or group of tasks. Project 2013 will adjust the project schedule accordingly.

To create a hierarchical structure to your project plan, you will create a WBS for the charity golf tournament.

PM2.01 **To Create a WBS**

a. Click **Gantt Chart** 📊 on the View Bar if necessary.

b. Select **Set tournament objectives** (Task 1). Press ⎀Insert⎀ to insert a new blank task. Enter the task name Tournament Initiation. Press ⎀Tab⎀ but do not set a task duration.

c. Select **Tasks 2-5**, and then click the **TASK** tab. In the Schedule group, click **Indent Task** ⤏. Notice the new task, Tournament Initiation (Task 1), becomes bold to identify it as a summary task. The duration of the summary task is determined by the durations of the subtasks (Tasks 2–5).

MODULE 1

SIDE NOTE

Insert Task

If you do not have an Insert key, use the Task 📊 button on the Insert group of the Task tab.

SIDE NOTE

Summary Tasks

Do not adjust the duration of a summary task; it is determined by subtasks. To adjust summary task durations, adjust subtask durations or relationships.

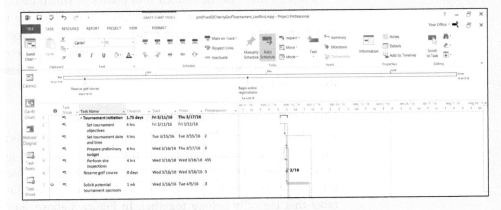

Figure 5   Summary task and subtasks

d.   Select **Reserve golf course** (Task 6). Press [Alt]+[Shift]+[→] to indent Task 6. Task 6 is now a subtask of Tournament Initiation.

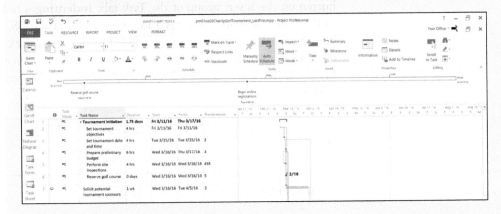

Figure 6   Task 6 as a subtask

e.   Select **Solicit potential tournament sponsors** (Task 7). In the Insert group of the TASK tab, click **Task** [icon] to insert a new blank task. Add the task name Tournament Promotion and press [Tab] but do not add a duration. Notice Tournament Promotion (Task 7) becomes a subtask of Tournament Initiation (Task 1).

f.   In the Schedule group of the TASK tab, click **Outdent Task** [icon] to promote Tournament Promotion (Task 7).

g.   Select **Tasks 8–11**, and in the Schedule group, click **Indent Task** [icon] to make Tasks 8–11 subtasks of Tournament Promotion (Task 7).

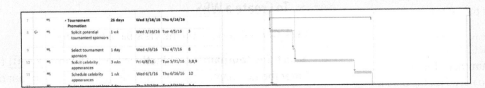

Figure 7   Tournament Promotion summary task and subtasks

h.   Select Task 12 through Task 14. In the Insert group, click **Summary** [icon] to insert a summary task. Add the summary task name Tournament Website and press [Tab].

i.   Click **Save** [icon].

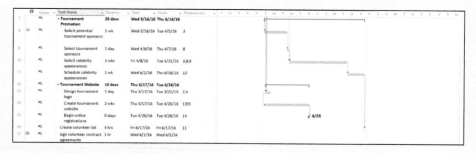

Figure 8   Project Work Breakdown Structure

CONSIDER THIS | **Why Create a Work Breakdown Structure?**

Have you ever written a report or a research paper? Did you create an outline to keep track of large amounts of information or to show a logical ordering of information before you actually started writing your paper? An outline for a written report is similar to a Work Breakdown Structure for a project plan.

Filtering a WBS in Gantt Chart and Network Diagram Views

Once a Work Breakdown Structure is created, you may want to temporarily hide project tasks. For example, if you organized your project by phases, you may only want the phase you are currently working in showing. In this case, you could collapse all other phases of the WBS to only view the tasks in the current phase. You can also perform a filter of the WBS to only show certain tasks.

PM2.02 **To Hide Tasks in a WBS**

a. Click **Tournament Promotion** (Task 7). Click the **Collapse arrow** ⬛ in the upper left-hand corner of the Task Name cell. The subtasks of Tournament Promotion (Task 7) are now hidden.

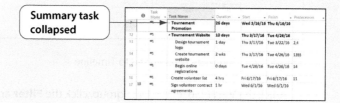

Figure 9   Work Breakdown Structure with summary task collapsed

b. Click the **Expand arrow** ▷ in the upper left-hand corner of the Task Name cell for Tournament Promotion (Task 7). The Tournament Promotion subtasks reappear.

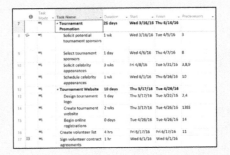

Figure 10   Work Breakdown Structure with summary task expanded

c. To filter Gantt Chart view, select the **VIEW** tab. In the Data group, click the **Filter** arrow, and then click **Summary Tasks**. Gantt Chart view is now filtered to show only summary tasks.

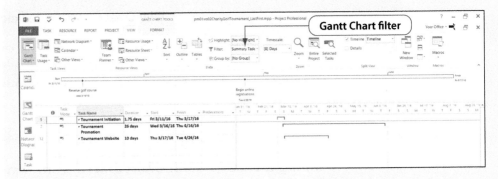

Figure 11   Filtered Gantt Chart

d. Click the **TASK** tab. Select the Summary tasks by highlighting the row selectors, and then in the Properties group, click **Add Task to Timeline** 🔲 to add the summary tasks to the Timeline.

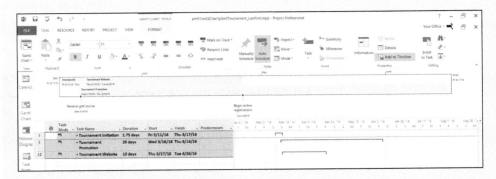

Figure 12   Summary tasks added to Timeline

e. Click the **VIEW** tab. In the Data group, click the **Filter** arrow, and then click **No Filter**. All summary tasks and subtasks reappear.

f. Click **Save** 🔲.

Displaying WBS Code in the Entry Table

When you create a WBS by including summary tasks, Project can assign a WBS code for each task. If you want to refer to tasks by a WBS code, which will give you more definition than using the task row, you can define the code and then add the code to the Entry table.

PM2.03 To Define and Display a WBS Code

a. Click the **TASK** tab if necessary, and then right-click the **Task Mode** column. Click **Hide Column**.

b. Right-click the **Task Name** column, and then click **Insert Column**.

c. Type **w**, and then click **WBS**. Double-click the WBS column border to resize the column width as necessary.

d. Click the **PROJECT** tab. In the Properties group, click **WBS**, and then click **Define Code** to activate the WBS Code Definition dialog box.

Figure 13   WBS Code Definition dialog box

e. To define the WBS code, in the first row of the table of the dialog box, click the **Sequence** list arrow, and then select **Uppercase Letters**. Click in the second row, and then click **Lowercase Letters**. Click in the third row, and then click **Numbers**.

Figure 14   WBS Code definition dialog box with code defined

f. Click **OK**.

Figure 15   Gantt Chart view with WBS column added

g. Click **Save** 🖫.

SIDE NOTE

Adjusting Column Width

You can also point to the right edge of a column title and then click and drag to the left or right to adjust the column width.

Create and Assign Project Resources

One of the main advantages of using project planning software such as Project 2013 is the ability to assign and track resources. Resources are the people, materials, or costs needed to complete project tasks. When you add resources in Project 2013, you are making them available to assign them to project tasks. Resources can be added in many views in Project 2013. However, the most common way of adding resources is by using Resource Sheet view, as shown in Figure 16.

Figure 16   Resource Sheet view

In **Resource Sheet view**, you can enter resource information in columns and rows to include information such as resource name, resource type, resource cost, and you can assign a calendar to a resource.

In the Resource Name column, you identify the name of the resource. For example, a resource could be Your Name. In the Type column, you identify whether a resource is a work, material, or cost resource. A Work resource is the person and equipment that needs to be used to complete a project task. For example, a chef hired to prepare the meal for the golf charity tournament is a resource; the equipment rented to prepare the meal is also a work resource. A Material resource is a consumable resource such as supplies. For example, golf tees would be a material resource. A Cost resource includes costs that are not based on work. For example, you may have to rent a tent for the staging area off the first tee of the golf course. The tent rental would be assigned as a cost resource.

The Initials column allows you to assign initials to a resource for identification instead of a longer resource name. For example, you could assign the initials of YN for Your Name and then display the initials in the Gantt chart to save space versus using the entire resource name. In the Group column, you can assign a group name to like resources. For example, you could assign the group name "Caddy" and then add this group name to all resources that are tournament caddies. You can then use the group name to sort or filter resources by the group name.

The Max column determines the maximum percentage of capacity a resource is available to work. By default, the Max Unit is 100%, which means the resource is available to work 100% of the time when assigned to a task. If you are only available to work half of the time on a project because you are assigned to other tasks at the resort, you would assign yourself a Max unit of 50%.

The Std. Rate, Ovt. Rate, and Cost/Use columns are associated with costs assigned to a resource. A cost is an expense associated with completing a task. Variable costs are costs that change based on amount used. For example, labor (work resource) is a variable cost because the amount earned may vary from person to person. Fixed costs can be related to resources but do not vary with use. For example, a fixed cost would be a one-time fee for renting an outdoor tent.

The Accrue column determines how costs will be applied to a task. Start means the cost would be paid at the start of the project. End means the cost would be paid at the end of the project. Prorated is the default and if assigned, costs would be accrued as the resource was working on the project task(s).

The Base column determines which calendar your resource will be assigned. From this calendar assignment, Project will determine working time and nonworking time of a resource. The Standard calendar is the default base calendar.

To create a resource calendar, select the resource and then:

1. Click the Resource tab.
2. Click Information 📇 in the Properties group.
3. On the General tab of the Resource Information dialog box, click Change Working Time.
4. Click the Work Weeks tab, and then click Details.
5. In the Details dialog box, select the Working times or Nonworking times button. Edit the From and To times as necessary. Click OK in the three dialog boxes to accept the change to the resource calendar.

The availability of the selected resource will now reflect the resource calendar.

Creating Project Resources

To keep track of who will help you complete the charity golf tournament project tasks, you have decided to add project team members into the Resource Sheet. You will add the project team members in Resource Sheet view and then assign resources to your project tasks. Since all project team members' tasks are part of their general job duties, you will not assign a resource cost to the tasks.

PM2.04 To Create Project Resources

a. Click the **TASK** tab. In the View group, click the **Gantt Chart** arrow.

Figure 17   Resource Sheet selection

b. Click **Resource Sheet** to open the Resource Sheet. In the first row of the Resource Sheet table, in the Resource Name column, enter your first and last name. Press Tab to assign the Type **Work** to the resource. Tab two more times and add your initials in the Initials column. Press Tab and enter the title Events in the Group column.

c. Add the resources into the indicated columns as follows.

Resource Name	Type	Initials	Group
Patti Rochelle	Work	PR	Events
Lesa Martin	Work	LM	Events
Thomas Vance	Work	TV	Events
Rosalinda Hill	Work	RH	Events
Barry Cheney	Work	BC	Golf
John Schilling	Work	JS	Golf
Jorge Cruz	Work	JC	Golf
Robin Sanchez	Work	RS	Chef

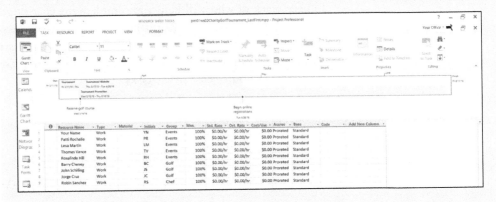

Figure 18   Resource Sheet view with resources added

d. Click the **VIEW** tab. In the Data group, click the **Group by** arrow, and then select **Resource Group**.

SIDE NOTE

Grouping Resources
Grouping resources can assist project managers in understanding resource allocations.

Figure 19   Resource Sheet with grouped resources

e. **Save** your project.

You can also add a new resource using the Task Information dialog box. In the Task Information dialog box, select the Resource tab, select the first blank row in the Resource name column, add a resource name and accompanying information, and click OK.

If you have ever been assigned to a team project, it is likely your teammate's availability differed from your availability. With this in mind, Project 2013 gives you the ability to create individual resource calendars that can be specifically designed for an individual resource. You can create a resource calendar in the Resource Information dialog box from the Properties group of the Resource tab. Once a resource calendar is created, it would be applied to a specific resource using the Resource Information dialog box. To open the Resource Information dialog box, click Information in the Properties group of the Resource tab.

Assigning Project Resources

Once resources are created, they must be assigned to tasks. Assigning a resource to a task means the resource is responsible for completing or overseeing the task. Project 2013 will assign the resource work and therefore the resource would be unavailable to complete other tasks at the same time. There are various ways of assigning project resources to tasks:

- The Assign Resources dialog box
- A cell in the Resource column arrow of the Entry table in Gantt Chart view
- The Resources tab in the Task Information dialog box
- The Task Work Form in Details view

The Assign Resources dialog box, used to assign resources to tasks, will remain open even when clicking outside of the dialog box to select tasks in the Entry Table. You can also create new resources in the Assign Resources dialog box. If you double-click a resource in the dialog box, it will open the Resource Information dialog box.

Now that you have created your project resources, you want to assign those resources to the project tasks. You will assign resources from the Assign Resources dialog box, the Resource column in the Entry table, and the Task Information dialog box.

PM2.05 To Assign Project Resources

a. Click **Gantt Chart** on the View Bar, and then drag the **split bar** to the right edge of the Resource Names column.

b. Click the **RESOURCE** tab, and then in the Assignments group, click **Assign Resources** to open the Assign Resources dialog box.

Figure 20   Assign Resources dialog box

SIDE NOTE
Resource Names in Gantt Chart
When you assign resources to tasks, notice the resource name will appear next to the Gantt bar in the Gantt chart.

c. With the Assign Resources dialog box still open, select **Set tournament objectives** (Task 2) in the Entry table. Click **Patti Rochelle** from the Assign Resources dialog box, and then click **Assign**.

d. Select **Set tournament date and time** (Task 3). Click **Patti Rochelle** from the Assign Resources dialog box, and then click **Assign**.

e. Select **Prepare preliminary budget** (Task 4). Again, click **Patti Rochelle** from the Assign Resources dialog box, and then click **Assign**.

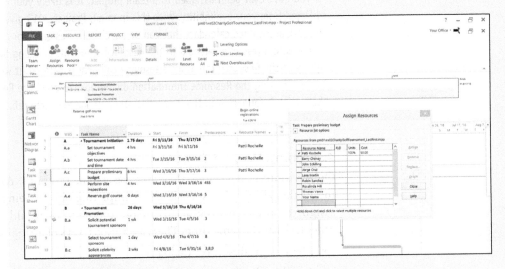

Figure 21 Resources assigned to tasks

f. Use the same procedure you used in Step e to make the following assignments.

Task 5	Perform site inspections	Your Name
Task 6	Reserve golf course	Your Name

g. Click **Close** in the Assign Resources dialog box.

Figure 22 Gantt chart with resource assignments

h. Click in the Resource Names cell for **Solicit potential tournament sponsors** (Task 8). Click the **arrow**, and then click in the check box for **Lesa Martin**. Press Enter to assign Lesa Martin to the task.

i. Click in the Resource Names cell for **Select tournament sponsors** (Task 9). Click the **arrow**, and then click in the check box for **Patti Rochelle**. Press Enter to assign Patti Rochelle to the task.

j. Click **Save** 🖫.

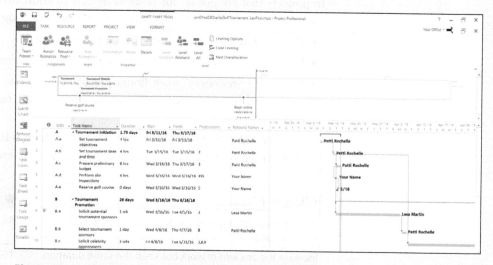

Figure 23 Gantt chart with additional resource assignments

Change Task Durations by Adding Resources

Task durations may change when resources are added. Therefore, you must understand how work is calculated in Project 2013. How Project 2013 calculates the duration of a task depends on if the task is effort driven or fixed duration. **Effort-driven scheduling** is the default method of scheduling in Project 2013 in which the duration of a task is shortened as resources are added or lengthened as resources are removed from a task; however, the amount of effort (work) necessary to complete a task remains unchanged. In other words, the more effort assigned to a task (units), the shorter the duration will be (even though the total work does not change). When you remove a resource from an effort-driven task, Project 2013 will lengthen the duration of the task. With effort-driven scheduling, Project 2013 calculates work using the following formula: W=D*U [Work (W)=Duration (D)*Units (U)].

Imagine a task that takes 8 hours to complete. If you add a resource to the task, Project 2013 will assign that resource 8 hours of work. But what if you assign two resources to complete the same task? The amount of work hours stays the same (8 hours); however, the calendar time needed to complete the task (duration) will shorten the duration by 4 hours because the two resources (units) will be working together to get the task done faster. This scenario is based on the assumption the task is effort driven.

- W=D*U or D=W/U
- 8=4*2 or 4=8/2

Although effort-driven scheduling is usually the default in Project 2013, your school or organization may have the default set differently. To turn on effort-driven scheduling when starting a project, on the File tab, click Options, and then click Schedule. Individual tasks can also be set to effort-driven scheduling by using the Task Information dialog box for each task. For example, in an effort-driven project schedule, you may want to change one task to non-effort driven because the duration of a task may actually stay the same even if additional resources are added.

If a project is not set to effort-driven scheduling, Project 2013 will calculate work differently when resources are added. Imagine a task that takes 8 hours to complete. If you add a resource to the task, Project 2013 will assign the resources 8 hours of work. But what if you assign two resources to complete the same task? The amount of work hours increases to 16 hours (8 hours for resource one and 8 hours for resource two).

In projects that are not set for tasks to default to effort driven, if you add an additional resource to a task, Project 2013 will offer you the following options:

- Reduce duration but keep the same amount of work

- Increase the amount of work but keep the same duration

- Reduce the resources' work hours per day (units) but keep the same duration and work. (For example, assign each resource 50% of the task work not to be completed consecutively.)

To understand these choices, refer to Table 1, which is based on a task with an 8-hour duration using $W = D*U$ (U1 = one resource, U2 = second resource).

8-Hour Task Duration	W	D	U1	U2
Reduce duration but keep the same amount of work (effort driven)	8h	4h	4h	4h
Increase the amount of work but keep the same duration (work consecutively)	16h	8h	8h	8h
Reduce the hours resources work per day (units) but keep the same duration and work (work separately)	8h	8h	4h	4h

Table 1   Calculating task work for effort-driven task

When a resource is assigned to more work than available working hours, the resource will be **overallocated**. Project managers know that overallocating resources may lead to project failure because the work will likely not get done in the time it was scheduled. Therefore, Project provides a leveling tool. **Leveling** is a process of correcting overallocated resources to ensure no resource is assigned more hours than available work hours.

REAL WORLD ADVICE   **Leveling of Resources**

If a project's team members are assigned more work than they have time for, not only may they have poor performance or burnout, it is also likely they won't be able to finish all the work assigned. If work doesn't get done on time, the project may not meet the schedule deadline and may also go over budget. Project managers may choose to manually level resources by changing resource assignments, removing resource assignments, shortening task durations, adjusting the work of a resource on a task, or adding additional resource assignments to tasks. Project managers may also decide to allow Project to level the resources using Project's leveling tools from the Resource tab.

Another way of leveling a project is by adding additional resources to a project to be sure the project is still completed on time. Adding additional resources to the project is called **crashing**. A project manager may also decide to crash a project to complete tasks faster than predicted to shorten the project's duration. Crashing a project may help to level a project or complete a project faster but may also cause the project to go over budget.

What Would You Do?

Have you ever fallen behind on studying for a test? If so, what did you do, pull an all-nighter? What if your project has fallen behind schedule? Or what if you want to finish the project earlier than predicted to get a jump on the competition? Project managers may decide to add additional resources to the project, knowing this will likely increase the project's budget.

Setting Your Project to Effort Driven

For the golf charity tournament, you believe your tasks will take less time to complete (duration) if you add additional resources to your tasks. Therefore, you want to set your project to schedule all tasks as effort driven unless otherwise specified.

PM2.06 To Set New Project Tasks to Effort-Driven

a. Click the **FILE** tab, and then click **Options**.

b. In the Project Options dialog box, click **Schedule** in the left pane.

c. Scroll down until you see the **Scheduling options for this project** section. If necessary, click the **New tasks are effort-driven** check box to set all new tasks as effort-driven tasks.

Figure 24　Project Options scheduling dialog box

d. Click **OK**, and then save your project.

Changing Task Durations with Resource Assignments

Now that new project tasks will be scheduled as effort driven, you will continue resource assignments for the remaining project tasks.

PM2.07 To Change Task Duration by Adding Resources

a. Click **Gantt Chart** 🔲 if necessary, and then click Design tournament logo (Task 13). Assign **Rosalinda Hill** to Task 13.

b. Double-click **Create tournament website** (Task 14) to open the Task Information dialog box. Click the **Resources** tab. Notice the duration on this task is two weeks (80 hours).

c. Click the first cell under the Resource Name heading, and then click the **Resource Name** arrow. Click **Thomas Vance** to add him as a resource to this task, and then click **OK**. Thomas is now assigned 80 hours of work on Create tournament website (Task 14).

d. In the Resource Names column of **Create tournament website** (Task 14), click the **Resource Names** arrow to also select Rosalinda Hill. Click **Rosalinda Hill,** and then press Enter.

e. Project will give an informational warning symbol. Click on the **warning symbol** to reveal the three selections for assigning the additional resource.

Figure 25   Resource assignment warning

f. Select **Reduce duration but keep the same amount of work**. Note the changes to the duration of Task 14 to one week versus the original two week duration. The total work is still 80 hours but the time needed to complete the work is cut in half because two resources are assigned.

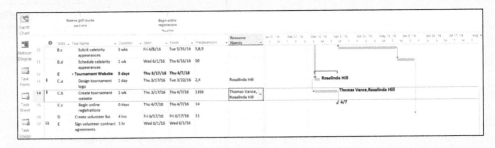

Figure 26   Duration changed with resource assignment

g. Click **Begin online registrations** (Task 15) and then assign **Patti Rochelle** to the task.

h. Double-click **Solicit celebrity appearances** (Task 10), and then click the **Advanced** tab. If necessary, click the **Effort driven** check box to set the task to effort driven. Click **OK**.

i. With **Task 10** still selected, click the **RESOURCE** tab, and then in the Assignments group, click **Assign Resources** 👥.

j. Using the Assign Resources dialog box, click **Your Name**, and then click **Assign**. Click **Patti Rochelle**, and then click **Assign**. Note the change in the duration from three weeks to one and a half weeks due to the task being effort driven.

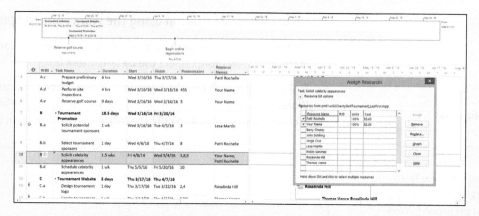

Figure 27   Task duration change

> **Troubleshooting**
>
> If the duration of Task 10 did not change to 1.5 weeks, make sure the task is set to effort driven by double-clicking the task, clicking the Advanced tab, and placing a check mark in front of Effort driven.

k. Click **Close** in the Assign Resources dialog box, and then save your project.

Using the Work Task Form in Split View

Understanding how Project 2013 is calculating task durations and task work can be confusing. Project managers often find it useful to use the Task Details Form in split screen view. The Task Details Form in Split View allows you to see exactly how Project is distributing the work on a task as shown in Figure 28.

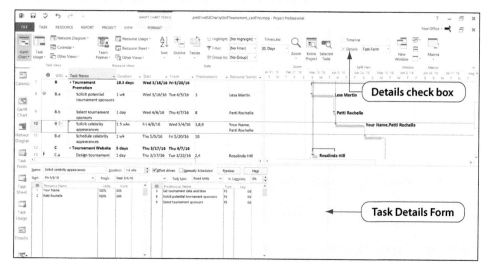

Figure 28   Task Details Form in Split View

PM2.08 To Change a Duration using the Work Form in Split View

a. Click **Solicit celebrity appearances** (Task 10) if necessary, and then click the **VIEW** tab. In the Split View group, select the **Details** check box.

b. Right-click the **Task Details Form** in the lower pane of Gantt Chart view, and then click **Work**. You see that you are assigned 60 hours of work and Patti Rochelle is also assigned 60 hours of work. You also note the task has a check mark in the Effort driven check box.

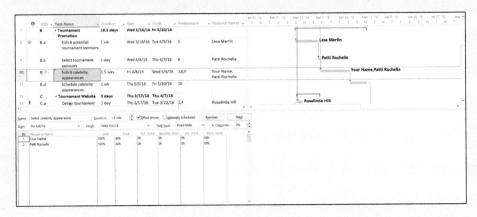

Figure 29   Work Form in Split View

c. In the Work form, click the **Next** button. **Schedule celebrity appearances** (Task 11) is now selected. Note the task has a 1-week duration (or 40 hours).

d. In the **Resource Name** column of the Work form, click in the first blank row in the Resource Name column. Click the arrow, and then click **Your Name**. Click in the blank row below Your Name, and then click **Barry Cheney**.

e. Click **OK** to assign both resources to this task. Notice in the Work form that both resources are assigned 40 hours of work. Although the task duration remains 1 week, the total work hours has doubled to 80 hours because the task is not effort driven.

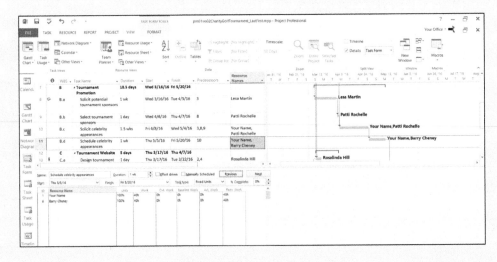

Figure 30   Work form with non-effort-driven task

f. Click in the **Work** cell of **Your Name row** in the Work form. Enter **10h** to change your work hours to 10 hours.

g. Click in the **Work** cell for **Barry Cheney**. Enter **30h** to change Barry's work hours to 30 hours. Click **OK**.

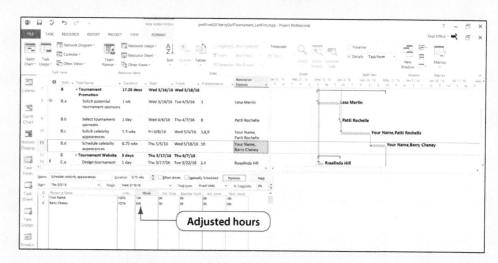

Figure 31   Resource work hours manually adjusted

h. Note the change in the duration from 1 week to .75 weeks. By manually changing the work hours, you are creating an assignment similar to an effort-driven task. Click **Next** five times.

i. Assign **Rosalinda Hill** to **Create volunteer list** (Task 16) and to **Sign volunteer contract agreements** (Task 17), and then click **OK**.

j. In the Split View group of the **VIEW** tab, close the split view by deselecting the **Details** check box, and then click **Save** 🖫.

SIDE NOTE
Removing Split View
To remove the Split View group, you can also double-click the split bar between the Entry table and the Work form.

View Resource Assignments in the Team Planner View

After assigning resources, project managers may want to view how project team members are being assigned at a point in the project. This can be done by using Project's team planner. **Team Planner** is a Project view that shows a project's resources and tasks assigned to each resource. Each resource name appears on a separate row. In Team Planner view, you can drag task assignments from one resource to another resource to make adjustments to the resource assignment(s). Tasks associated with the individual resources appear on the same row as the resource name. Unassigned tasks appear at the bottom of the Team Planner view window. Resources identified in red are overallocated resources.

SIDE NOTE
Resource Assignments in Team Planner View
You can adjust resource assignments by clicking on a task in Team Planner view and dragging the task to a new resource.

PM2.09 **To View Resource Assignments in Team Planner View**

a. Click the **VIEW** tab, and then in the Resource Views group, click **Team Planner** 🖼 to open Team Planner view.

b. Right-click **Your Name**, and then click **Scroll to Task** 🔍.

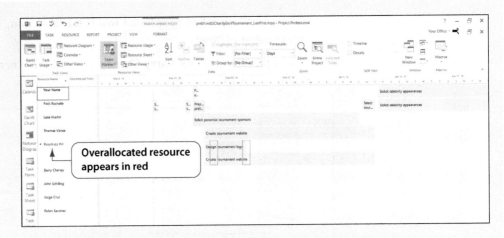

Figure 32   Team Planner view

c.   View the tasks assigned to you in Team Planner view. Use the horizontal scroll bar to view all tasks you are assigned to. View the tasks assigned to others in Team Planner view.

d.   Click **Gantt Chart** on the View Bar.

REAL WORLD ADVICE   **Project Schedule and Resource Assignments**

As you have learned, a project's schedule is calculated by Project based on things such as a project's calendar, task durations, task relationships, and resources assignments. However, project managers have the ultimate decision-making authority on the project's overall schedule. If Project is not creating a project schedule that makes sense to the project's needs, a project manager should review how the schedule is being created and make adjustments to the project calendar, task durations, task relationships, or resources assignments accordingly.

Enhance a Project Schedule with Elapsed Duration and Recurring Tasks

If you assign a task a duration of 48 hours, Project will schedule that task for 6 days of work (48 hours divided by an 8-hour work day). However, assume a task in your project needs 48 hours total without regard to the Project calendar. If this is the case, Project 2013 allows you to assign elapsed duration times. **Elapsed durations** ignore any project or resources working and nonworking times and schedules the task(s) to 24 hours a day.

Adding Elapsed Durations

You want to allow the online registration to be open for 6 weeks. Therefore, you will add the task and assign the task a 6-week duration to give participants time to register for the event. However, the project calendar allows for only 16 hours of work each week and does not account for the fact that participants can register any time of the day. Therefore, a 6-week duration will assign the task to last over 3 months, but you only want the registration open for 6 weeks. You decide to change the duration to elapsed time to accurately reflect how long you want online registration to remain open.

PM2.10 To Set a Task Duration to Elapsed Time

a. Click **Create volunteer list** (Task 16), and then press Insert to insert a new task row. Add the task name Accept online registrations. Press Tab and assign the task a duration of **10 weeks**. Press Tab three times and enter 15 to assign a predecessor of Task 15. Press Tab. Note this task takes six months to complete.

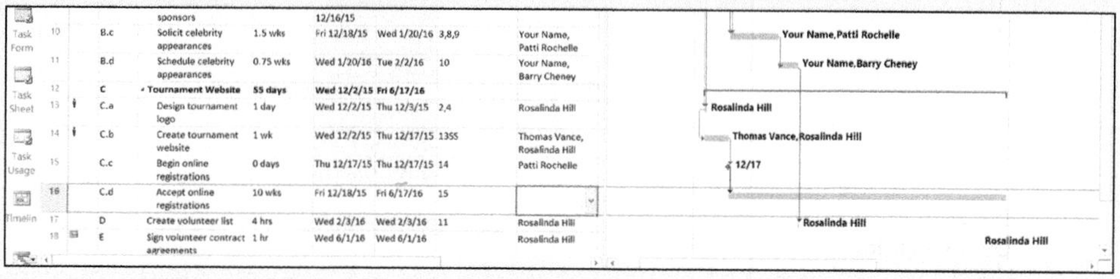

Figure 33 Task duration

b. Click in the **Duration** column of Task 16, and then change the duration of the task to 10ew. Note the change to task Start date of this task. Making the duration an elapsed time more accurately reflects the assignment of that task.

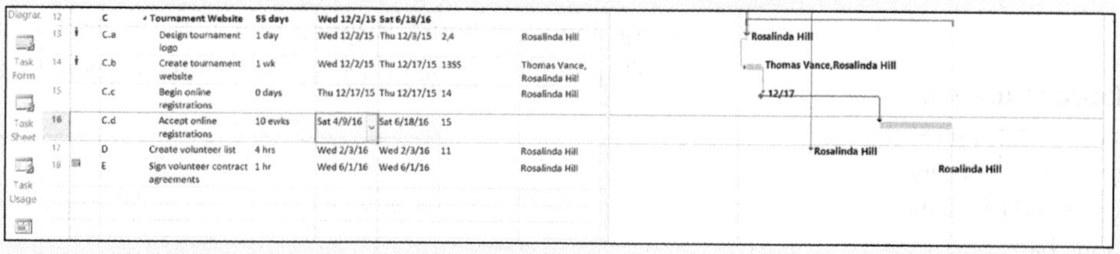

Figure 34 Elapsed duration assigned to a task

SIDE NOTE

Overallocation

The overallocated indicator will appear on all tasks assigned to an overallocated resource.

c. Add **Your Name** as the resource to Task 16. The graphic in the Indicators column shows overallocation. By assigning yourself to this task you have overallocated yourself.

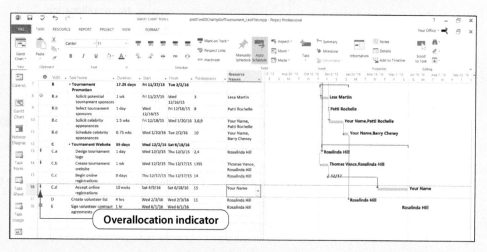

Figure 35 Entry table with overallocated resource

d. With Task 16 still selected, open the Work form in **Split View** by clicking **Details** in the Split View group of the **VIEW** tab. Note you are assigned to 1,680 hours of work on Task 16.

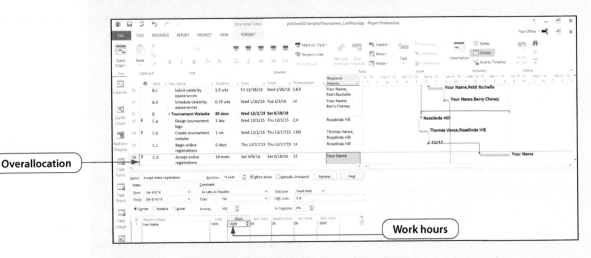

Figure 36 Work Form in Split View

SIDE NOTE

Elapsed Duration
A task assigned an elapsed duration is displayed as a dotted line in the Gantt chart.

e. Change the work hours assigned to you to **0h** since you do not need to spend time actually completing the task. Click **OK**. Note the overallocation on Task 16 is removed.

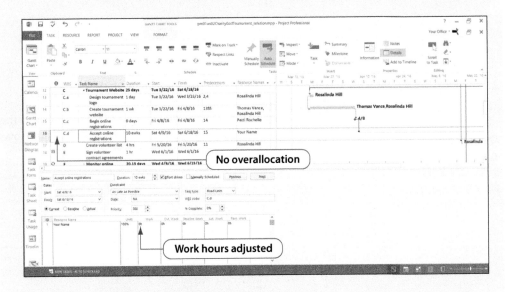

Figure 37 Overallocation of Task 16 removed

f. Click the **VIEW** tab. From the Split View group, deselect the **Details** check box to remove the split form.

g. Click **Save** .

Adding a Recurring Task

There are also circumstances where you may do the same task over and over, such as a weekly status meeting. Tasks that have a regular occurrence can be entered into the Project software as recurring tasks. A **recurring task** is a task that repeats at regular intervals. For example, you may want to monitor online registrations every Wednesday to be sure the tournament is receiving enough registrations. Instead of setting up separate tasks each week, you could create a recurring task.

PM2.11 To Create a Recurring Task

a. Click in the Task Name column of row 19, the first blank row of the Entry table. On the TASK tab, in the Insert group, click the **Task** button arrow. Click **Recurring Task** to open the Recurring Task Information dialog box.

Figure 38   Recurring Task Information dialog box

b. Enter the Task Name Monitor online registrations. Enter a duration of **1h**.

c. If necessary, click **Weekly** under the Recurrence pattern. Set the task to recur every **1 week** on **Wednesday**. Set the recurrence pattern to start on **April 6, 2016** and end on **June 15, 2016**. Apply the **Standard Calendar** to the task.

Figure 39   Recurring Task Information dialog box with task information

d. Click **OK**. A Recurring Task indicator appears in the Indicators column.

e. Click the **VIEW** tab, and then in the Zoom group click **Entire Project** to view the entire project plan in the Gantt chart.

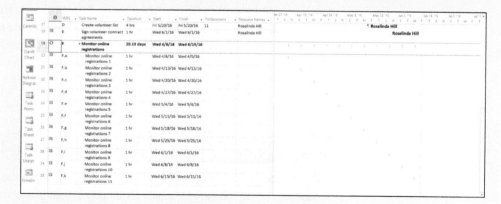

Figure 40   Entry table with recurring task information

f. Click the **Collapse** ⊿ button in the upper left-hand corner of the name box of the recurring task in row 19 to collapse the individual tasks.

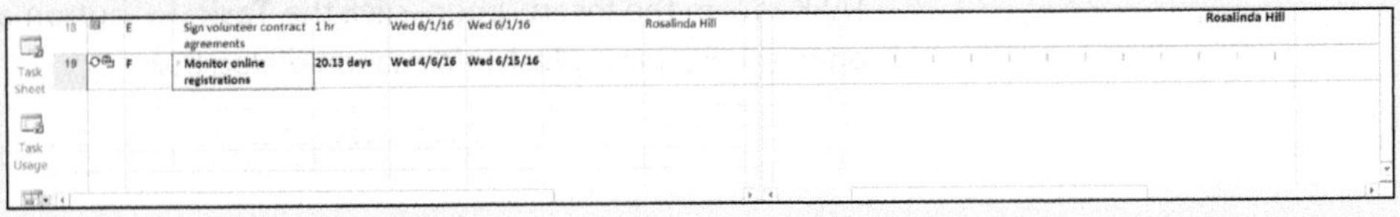

Figure 41 Recurring task collapsed

g. **Save** your project.

Sharing Project Information

Communication is an integral part of a project manager's duties when managing projects. If a project manager is using Project 2013, project reports can be created. Project 2013 information can also be copied and pasted into other applications such as an Excel spreadsheet or a Word table. Information can also be exported to other applications or imported from other applications. Projects can be linked to other projects as well. Regardless of which method a project manager decides to use to share information, frequent project communication is good practice to be sure the entire project and project team stay on task.

Create Project Reports

The reporting features of Project 2013 have a new graphical appearance and many formatting capabilities. The reports now feature charts and images that better represent your project at a glance. You can add or remove elements in reports to fit your reporting needs. Project 2013 gives project managers dozens of pre-loaded reports that can be used immediately. Not only are these charts available, but they can also be customized to meet the project reporting needs. If a project manager does not find a report that works for a project, custom reports can also be created. Project allows for individual control of reports, from black and white to colors as well as chart effects.

Most of the reports available in Project are based on project status. To display the status of a project, a baseline must be set and the project is tracked. A baseline is a record of each task at a point in time from which you will track project progress. **Tracking** is recording the actual progress of the project's tasks (for example, identifying a task as completed or partially done). Baselines are set on the Project tab, and task tracking is done in the Schedule group of the Task tab.

REAL WORLD ADVICE	Setting a Project Baseline

If your supervisor asks you how the project is going, you want to be sure to have an answer. Project managers who want the ability to run project reports to update the project status and compare where the project is compared to where the project should be will set a project baseline. As a snapshot of the original plan of the project, a baseline allows you to compare what should be happening with your project versus what is actually happening with your project.

Table 2 defines the five pre-determined Dashboard reports. Dashboard reports display project progress.

Report name	Description
Burndown	This reports how much work you have completed and how much work you have left to complete.
Cost Overview	This report displays the current cost status of your project and its top-level (Summary) to help you determine if your project is staying on budget.
Project Overview	This report displays how much of the project is complete as well as any upcoming milestones and tasks that are past due (late tasks).
Upcoming Tasks	This report displays the work that has been done during the current week, the status of any remaining tasks that were due, and which tasks may be starting in the next week.
Work Overview	This report displays how much work you have completed and how much you have left (such as burndown) as well as remaining availability of work resources.

Table 2 Dashboard reports

Creating Project Reports

In addition to Dashboard reports , there are also Resources , Costs , In Progress , and Custom reports . Although you have not set a project baseline and therefore have not started tracking your project, you still can explore the available reports for your project.

PM2.12 To View Reports in Project

a. Click the **REPORT** tab. In the View Reports group, click the **Resources** arrow and select **Resource Overview**. Notice the graphical nature of the report and the features available to customize reports on the REPORT TOOLS DESIGN tab.

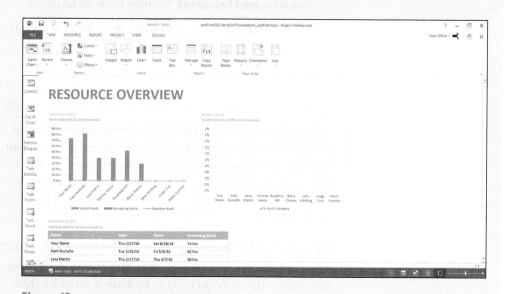

Figure 42 Resource Overview report

b. Click the **REPORT** tab. In the View Reports group, click the **Resources** arrow and select **Overallocated Resources** to view the overallocation for Rosalinda Hill.

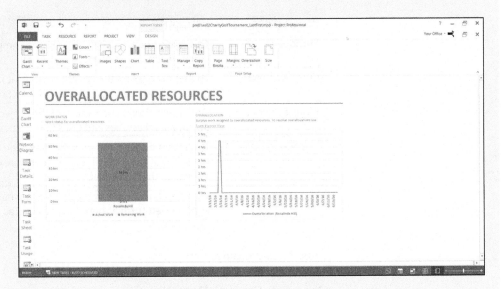

Figure 43 Overallocated Resources report

c. Click **Gantt Chart** [icon] from the View Bar, and then select **Create tournament website** (Task 14).

d. Click the **VIEW** tab. In the Split View group, select the **Details** check box to open the split form.

e. Change the work hours for Rosalinda Hill to 10h. Click **OK.**

f. Click the **VIEW** tab. In the Split View group, deselect the Details check box to remove the split view.

g. Click the **REPORT** tab. In the View Reports group, click the **Resources** arrow and select **Overallocated Resources**. You note there are no longer overallocated resources.

h. Click **Gantt Chart** from the View Bar, and then click **Save** [icon].

Copy and Paste Project Information to Other Applications

A project manager is not limited to sharing project information through Project's reports. Project 2013 information can be shared by copying and pasting project information into another application such as Excel or Word. Since Excel is similar to Project's Entry table, pasting information into Excel will create a worksheet with columns and rows of data. When you paste information into Word, however, project information will be pasted into a table format.

Copying and Pasting Project Information to Excel and Word

You want to share your project information with other project team members who do not have knowledge of Project 2013. To make it easier for them to view the project's information, you will copy the information and then paste into Excel and Word.

To Copy Data into an Excel Workbook and a Word Document

a. Click the **Select All** button in the upper left-hand corner of the Entry table.

Select All

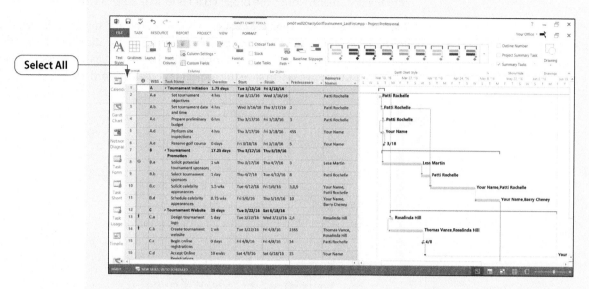

Figure 44   Entry table Select All button

b. Click the **TASK** tab, and then in the Clipboard group, click **Copy** 📋.

c. While keeping your Project 2013 file open, locate and open **Excel 2013**. Select **Blank workbook** to create a blank Excel workbook.

d. If necessary, click in cell A1 and press CTRL+V to paste the project's entry table data into Excel.

e. To adjust the column widths, right-click the column header for Column B. Click **Column Width**, and then enter **35**.

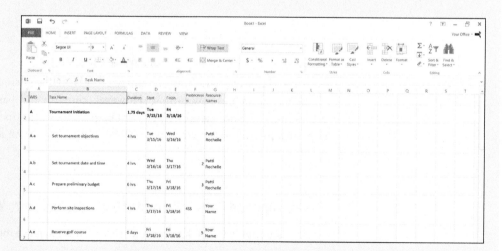

Figure 45   Project data pasted into an Excel workbook

f. Click the **FILE** tab, and then click **Save**. Click **Computer**, and then click **Browse**. Navigate to the location where you are storing your files. In the Save As dialog box, click in the File name box and enter pm01ws02CharityGolfTournament_LastFirst using your last and first name. Click **Save** to save the project task data in Excel format. Click **Close** ❎ to close Excel 2013.

g. Locate and open **Word 2013**. Select **Blank document** to create a blank Word document.

h. On the HOME tab, in the Clipboard group, click **Paste** 📋 to paste your project's data into the document. Notice the project data is formatted as a Word table.

i. Click the **FILE** tab, and then click **Save**. Click **Computer**, and then click **Browse**. Navigate to the location where you store your files. In the Save As dialog box, click in the File name box and enter pm01ws02CharityGolfTournament_LastFirst using your last and first name. Click **Save** 🖫 to save the project task data in Word format.

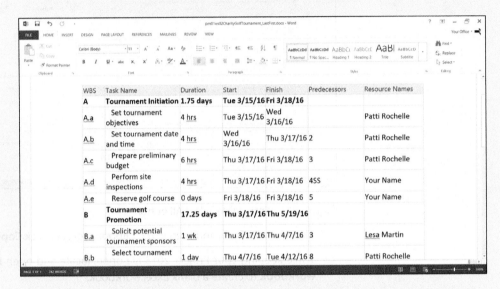

Figure 46   Project data pasted into a Word document as a table

j. Click **Close** ✖ to close Word, and return to your **pm01ws02CharityGolfTournament_LastFirst.mmp** Project file.

Copying Project Information as a Picture

Copying and pasting data from the Entry table works well since the Entry table is similar to Excel's column and row format. However, copying and pasting project data does not work well in Calendar view or Network Diagram view. In this case, you may want to copy and paste a picture of the view into another application such as Microsoft Word.

PM2.14 To Copy and Paste a Picture of Calendar View into Word

a. Click **Calendar** view 📅. If necessary, click **Month** to view a month of your project plan.

b. If necessary, scroll in the calendar until you display the month of May 2016.

c. On the TASK tab, in the Clipboard group, click the **Copy** button arrow, and then click **Copy Picture** from the menu. The Copy Picture dialog box opens.

Figure 47 Copy Picture dialog box

SIDE NOTE

Microsoft PowerPoint
You could also paste a picture of your project into a PowerPoint presentation.

d. Click **OK** to accept the default settings.

e. Once again, open **Microsoft Word 2013**, and then select **Blank document** to create a blank Word document.

f. On the HOME tab, in the Clipboard group, click the **Paste** button to paste Project Calendar view data into the document as a picture.

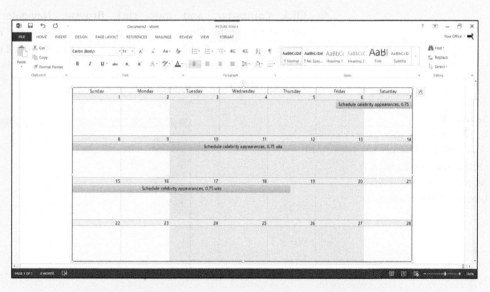

Figure 48 Project Calendar view data pasted as a picture into a Word document

g. Click the **FILE** tab, and then click **Save As**. Click **Computer**, and then click **Browse**. Navigate to the location where you store your files. Click in the File name box and type pm01ws02CharityGolfTournamentCalendar_LastFirst using your last and first name.

h. Click **Save** to save the project Calendar data in Word format, and then click **Close** [X] to close Word.

Share Project Information with Microsoft Excel

There may be situations in which you need to share project information with other members of your project team or organization who do not have access to Project 2013. In this case, you can export your project data into Excel. When you begin the exporting process, the Export Wizard will take you through a series of steps to export all fields for project categories into a new format.

Exporting Project Information to Excel

You want to share your project information with your project team, but you have been informed some do not have access to Project 2013 software. Therefore, you decide to export your project data into Excel so that your project team can also see the project's tasks.

PM2.15 **To Export Project Information into Excel**

a. Click **Gantt Chart** [icon] on the View Bar to return to Gantt Chart view. Select the **FILE** tab, and then click **Save As**.

b. Click **Computer**, and then click **Browse**. Navigate to the location where you store your files. In the File name section, enter the project name pm01ws02CharityGolfTournamentExport_LastFirst. Click the **Save as type** arrow, and then click **Excel Workbook.**

c. Click **Save**. The Export Wizard dialog box opens.

SIDE NOTE

Save as PDF

You can also save your Project file as a PDF by clicking the File tab, Save As, and in the Save as type: box, select PDF Files (.pdf).

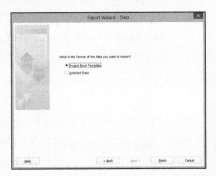

Figure 49 Export Wizard dialog box

d. Click the **Next** button. Click the **Project Excel Template** button.

Figure 50 Export Wizard – Data dialog box

e. Click **Finish**. Click **OK** to close the dialog box warning. Your project data is exported to Excel.

f. Use Windows Explorer to navigate to the location where you store your data files. Select **pm01ws02CharityGolfTournamentExport_LastFirst.xlsx** to open the charity golf tournament file in Excel.

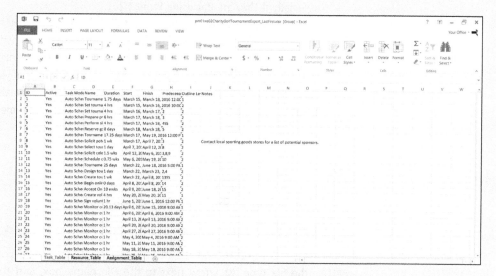

Figure 51 Excel workbook with exported Project 2013 data

g. Explore the sheet tabs, and then **Close** ☒ Excel. Return to your **pm01ws02CharityGolfTournament_LastFirst.mpp** project file.

QUICK REFERENCE	**Exporting Project Data to Excel 2013**

1. Select the File tab, and then click Save As.
2. Click Browse to navigate to where you store your files.
3. Click the Save as type arrow, and then click Excel Workbook.
4. Click Save to open the Export Wizard dialog box.
5. Click the Next button.
6. Click the Project Excel Template button.
7. Click Finish.

Importing Project Information from Excel

Although information can be copied into Project from another application such as Excel, importing information into Project is more flexible by allowing for data to be imported that does not exactly match. By importing data from Excel, you can use the Import/Export Wizard to assist in bringing in field data into a new project or a current project.

It is not uncommon for projects to be a collaboration of efforts between more than one organization or project team. For example, a project may rely on collaboration with an external vendor. Whenever working with someone outside your organization, it may be difficult to obtain their project schedule in a format that works with your project, especially if they are not using Project 2013.

If an external vendor is using Project 2013 for its schedule needs, the vendor may not want to give you its entire project schedule because it may contain costing and salary information that is private to its organization. If this is the case, you can request an Excel file with tasks and start and finish dates that you can then import directly into your project plan. If the vendor is also using Project 2013, it may actually be exporting the data from Project 2013 to Excel to get you an Excel file, which you can then import back into Project 2013.

PM2.16 To Import Project Information from Excel

a. With your Project file open, click the **FILE** tab, and then click **Open**.

b. Click **Computer**, and then navigate to the location of your student data files. Click the file type list arrow next to the File name box, and then click **Excel Workbook.** Click **pm01ws02CharityGolfTournamentTasks.xlsx**, and then click **Open** to open the Import Wizard dialog box.

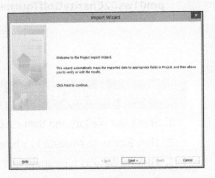

Figure 52   Import Wizard dialog box

c. Click **Next** to open the Import Wizard – Map dialog box and if necessary, click **New map**.

Figure 53   Import Wizard – Map dialog box

d. Click **Next** to open the Import Wizard – Import Mode dialog box. Click **Append the data to the active project**.

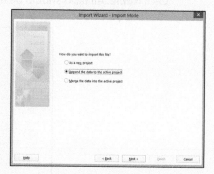

Figure 54   Import Wizard – Import Mode dialog box

e. Click **Next** to open the Import Wizard – Map Options dialog box. Click **Tasks** and if necessary click **Import includes headers**.

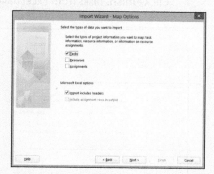

Figure 55   Import Wizard – Map Options dialog box

f. Click **Next** to open the Import Wizard – Task Mapping dialog box.

g. In the Import Wizard – Task Mapping dialog box, click the arrow on the **Source worksheet name** and click **TaskData**.

Excel sheet mapped to TaskData

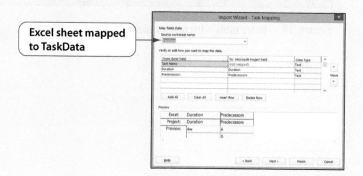

Figure 56   Import Wizard – Task Mapping dialog box

SIDE NOTE

Finding Column Names

When searching for column names, you can type the first letter of a column name to filter for only columns starting with that letter.

h. In the **To: Microsoft Project Field**, view the Task Name row that has the text (not mapped). Click the **(not mapped)** field list arrow, and then scroll until you see Name. Click **Name**. All tasks should be mapped.

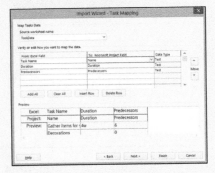

Figure 57   Import Wizard – Task Mapping dialog box with all tasks mapped

i. Click **Finish**. Tasks from Excel have been imported into your project starting at row 31.

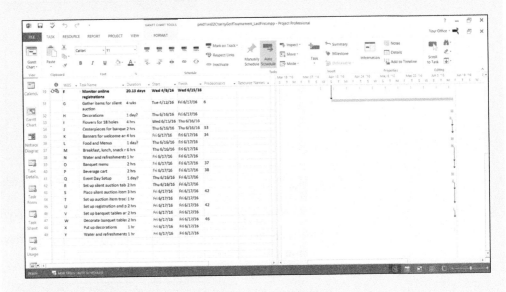

Figure 58   Entry table with tasks imported

j. **Save** your project.

QUICK REFERENCE | Importing Excel 2013 Data into Project

1. With a Project file open, click the File tab, and then click Open.
2. Navigate to the location where you store your files. Click the file type list arrow in the Open dialog box, and then click Excel Workbook.
3. Click the Excel workbook from which you want to import data, and then click Open.
4. Click Next.
5. In the Import Wizard – Map dialog box, click the New map option button, and then click Next.
6. In the Import Wizard – Import Mode dialog box, click Append the data to the active project, and then click Next.
7. In the Import Wizard – Map Options dialog box, click Tasks and Assignments, and if necessary, click Import includes headers, and then click Next.
8. In the Import Wizard – Task Mapping dialog box, click the arrow on the Source worksheet name, and click Sheet1—or other sheet name that contains the data you wish to import.
9. Verify or edit how you want to map the data portion. All tasks should be mapped.
10. Click Finish.

Adjusting Imported Project Tasks

Imported tasks may not have the proper formatting, task relationships, or resource assignments. Therefore, you will modify the imported tasks to meet your project's needs.

PM2.17 To Adjust the Imported Project Tasks from Excel

a. Select the task names in rows **31-49**. Click the **FORMAT** tab, and then in the Columns group, click **Wrap Text** 🖺 twice.

b. Click the **TASK** tab. Select **Tasks 33-35**, and then in the Schedule group, click **Indent Task** 🗗 to make the tasks subtasks of Decorations (Task 32).

c. Select **Tasks 37-40**, and then in the Schedule group, click **Indent Task** 🗗 to make the tasks subtasks of Food and Menus (Task 36).

d. Select **Tasks 42-49**, and then in the Schedule group, click **Indent Task** 🗗 to make the tasks subtasks of Event Day Setup (Task 41).

e. Click **Gather items for silent auction** (Task 31). Note the WBS code is inaccurate. Click the **PROJECT** tab, click **WBS**, click **Renumber**, be sure **Entire project** is selected, and then click **OK**. Click **Yes**.

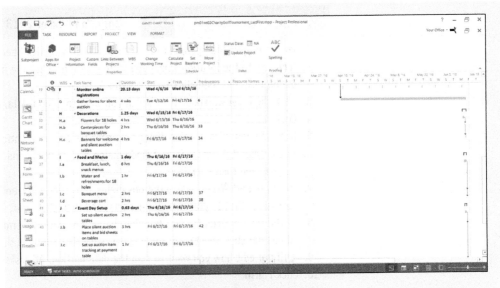

Figure 59   Imported tasks in a Work Breakdown Structure

SIDE NOTE

Effort-driven Tasks

Remember, new tasks have been set to effort-driven scheduling.

f.   Assign resources to the imported tasks as shown below.

WBS Code	Task Name	Resource
	Decorations	
H.a	Flowers for 18 holes	Your Name
H.b	Centerpieces for banquet tables	Your Name
H.c	Banners for welcome and silent auction tables	Your Name
	Food and Menus	
I.a	Breakfast, lunch, and snack menus	Robin Sanchez
I.b	Water and refreshments for 18 holes	Thomas Vance
I.c	Banquet menu	Robin Sanchez
I.d	Beverage cart	Thomas Vance
	Event Day Setup	
J.a	Set up silent auction tables	John Schilling
J.b	Place silent auction items and bid sheets on tables	Lesa Martin
J.c	Set up auction item tracking at payment table	Patti Rochelle
J.d	Set up registration and payment welcome table	John Schilling
J.e	Set up banquet tables and chairs	Barry Cheney, Jorge Cruz
J.f	Decorate banquet tables	Patti Rochelle, Your Name
J.g	Put up decorations	Rosalinda Hill
J.h	Water and refreshments placed at 18 holes for the golfers	Jorge Cruz

Table 3 Resource Assignments

g.   Select Tasks **37-40**, and then in the Properties group of the TASK tab, click **Information** to open the Multiple Task Information dialog box. Click the **Advanced** tab. Change the Constraint type to **As Soon As Possible**.

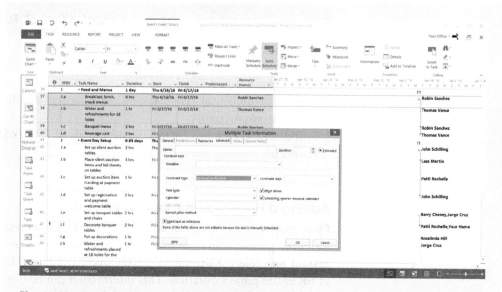

Figure 60 Multiple Task Information dialog box

SIDE NOTE

Task Constraints

Selecting multiple tasks to apply the same constraint can save you time over applying a constraint individually.

h. Click **OK**. Select **Tasks 33-35**. In the Properties group of the TASK tab, click **Information** to open the Multiple Task Information dialog box. Click the **Advanced** tab. Change the Constraint type to **Finish No Later Than** and set a Constraint date of **6/1/16**. Click **OK**. Note the calendar indicators in the Indicators column.

i. Click in the Resource Names column for Task 31, Gather items for silent auction. Assign **Thomas Vance, Patti Rochelle, Lesa Martin**, and **Your Name**. Select the **VIEW** tab, and then click the **Details** check box to add Split form view. Set the Work hours to **0** for each of the resources. Click **OK**. This removes the overallocation of these resources.

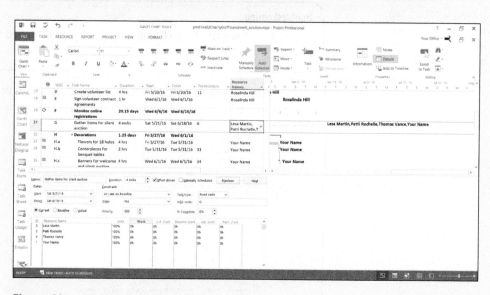

Figure 61 Work Form in Split View

j. Select Task 14, **Create tournament website**. Set the Work hours to **0** for **Rosalinda Hill**. Click **OK**. This removes the overallocation of all project resources. Close the split view. Click **Save** 🗗.

If you are using Project 2013 for your project planning, it is possible you are also using Microsoft Outlook for your email, contacts manager, tasks manager, and daily calendaring. If you are keeping project tasks in Outlook, it is possible for you to bring those tasks into your project plan instead of having to retype the tasks.

1. With your project plan open, click the Task tab.
2. In the Insert group, click the Task button arrow.
3. Click Import Outlook Tasks.
4. In the Import Outlook Tasks dialog box, click the expand button for the Folder: Tasks to display tasks in Outlook.
5. Click the check box for each task you want to import (or click Select all to select all tasks).
6. Click OK.

Adding a Project Summary Task

Once project tasks have been added, a WBS has been created, and project resources are assigned, project managers may want to view overall project information. It is often helpful for project managers to see the overall start and finish date of a project as well as the entire project duration. This information can be displayed at the top of the Entry table by adding a project summary task bar. A **project summary task** bar summarizes the timeline of your project and displays the total duration of your project. The same information can be found in the Project Information dialog box.

PM2.18 To Add a Project Summary Task

SIDE NOTE

Project Summary Task
The total duration of the project summary task is total hours worked represented in days, not total calendar days.

a. In Gantt Chart view, click the **GANTT CHART TOOLS FORMAT** tab. In the Show/Hide group, click **Project Summary Task**. View the project summary task bar (Task 0) in the Entry table and the Gantt chart.

> **Troubleshooting**
> If you do not see the Project Summary Task, you may need to scroll up until you see Row 0.

b. Click in the Task Name cell of **Task 0** to select it, and then press F2 on your keyboard to switch into Edit mode. Backspace the summary task name and enter the new name of **Charity Golf Tournament**.

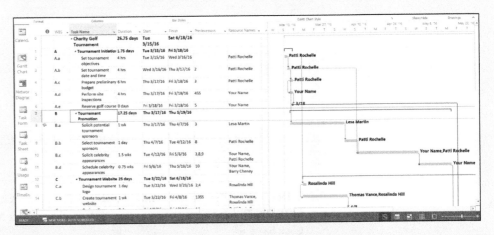

Figure 62   Project summary task

c. Click the **PROJECT** tab. In the Properties group, click **Project Information** [icon] to open the Project Information dialog box.

d. Click the **Statistics** button. View the project statistics and note they are the same as displayed on the project summary task.

Figure 63   Project Statistics

e. Click **Close** on the Project Statistics dialog box, and then click **Save** 🖫 and close your Project 2013 file.

Linking Excel Data to Project

Instead of copying, pasting, importing, or exporting data, there may be situations in which you want to link data to Project 2013 so you do not create a copy of the data. Another advantage of linking data is that if the data is updated in the source document (such as Excel), it is automatically updated in the destination file (such as Project) or vice versa. If data is updated in the source document but the destination document is closed, the destination document will be updated the next time it is opened.

A disadvantage of linking files is that the source file and the destination file must accompany each other if they are emailed, moved, or shared. Otherwise, you will "break a link" and get an error in the destination file. Another disadvantage is that you cannot create a map as you can when you import data into Project.

QUICK REFERENCE	Linking Excel Data to Project

1. Select and copy the data in Excel you want to link to Project.
2. In Project, click a cell in the Entry table where you wish to insert the data.
3. Select the Task tab.
4. In the Clipboard group of the Task tab, click the Paste button list arrow, and then click Paste Special.
5. Click Paste Link and select Microsoft Excel Worksheet.
6. Click OK.

Data linked to another source is indicated by a link graphic in the lower right-hand corner of a cell.

Use and Create Project Templates

A **Project template** is a Project file that contains sample project information such as tasks, durations, resources, and other project data. Templates can help you get started with your project if you are new to the Project 2013 software or the project management process. Templates can also help create consistency in your organization if projects are based on a standard template.

Creating a Project Plan from an Existing Project Template

When you opened a blank project in Workshop 1, you were opening the Blank Project template. This template has standards (defaults) in place such as project Start date, project manually scheduled, etc.

PM2.19 To Begin a Project from a Project Template

a. Click **FILE** if necessary, and then click **New**.

> **Troubleshooting**
> If the Project 2013 software is closed, you will need to reopen Project 2013.

b. In the right pane of the New window, click in the **Search** box and enter simple project plan. Press Enter. The Simple project plan template appears.

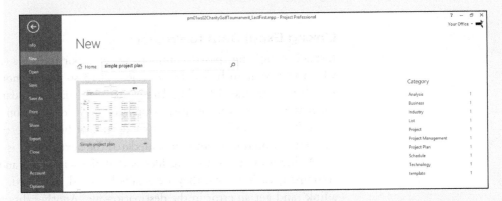

Figure 64   New project window with Simple project plan template

c. Click the **Simple project plan** icon to open the Simple project plan template window. Note how you can preview the template before downloading it.

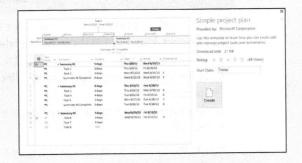

Figure 65   Simple project plan template preview window

d. In the Simple project plan window, click **Create**.

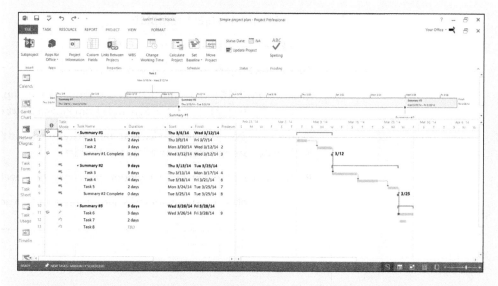

Figure 66   Simple project plan in Gantt Chart view

e. Explore the newly created project plan. Note the Summary task and subtask structure. Also view the notes in the Indicators column. Note some tasks are set to schedule manually while others are set to auto scheduled.

f. Click the **FILE** tab, and then click **Save As**. Click **Computer**, and then click **Browse**. Navigate to the location where you are saving your files.

g. In the Save As dialog box, click in the **File** name box, type pm01ws02SimpleProjectPlan_LastFirst using your last and first name. Click **Save** 🔲, and then **close** the project file.

Creating a Custom Project Template

Although there are many Project templates to choose from, they may not fit your project needs. Therefore, you can create a project plan and then save your plan as a template to use on future projects.

CONSIDER THIS | **Would You Like to Save Time Planning a Project?**

Do you have a routine for doing something such as getting ready for school? Or do you take the same route to work each day because it is the quickest way with the least amount of traffic? It is likely you follow the routine or take the same route to save yourself time. Think of a Project template as a fast route to beginning a project.

Since Painted Paradise Resort does a lot of event planning, you have decided to create a project template for planning events.

To Create a Project Template

a. Click **FILE** if necessary, and then click **New**.

b. Click **Blank Project** to open a new blank project.

c. Click the **PROJECT** tab, and then in the Properties group, click Project Information to verify the project is set to Schedule from Project **Start date**. Click **OK**.

d. On the Status bar, click **New Tasks: Manually Scheduled**, and then click **Auto Scheduled - Tasks dates are calculated by Microsoft Project**.

e. If necessary, set the new project window to display the View Bar and the Timeline.

f. Enter in the following summary tasks and subtasks, but do not supply durations.

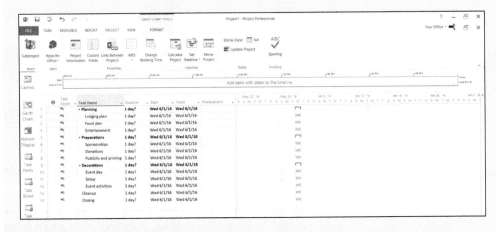

Figure 67 Template tasks

g. Click the **FILE** tab and click **Save As**. Click **Computer**, and then navigate to where you store your files. In the File name box enter pm01ws02EventTemplate_LastFirst.

h. Click the **Save as type** arrow, click **Project Template**.

Figure 68 Save As dialog box

i. Click **Save** to open the Save As Template dialog box. Since you have only added the summary task information, you do not need to check any of the boxes on the Save As Template dialog box. Click **Save**. The template is now saved and the template .mpt file extension should appear in the title bar.

j. Click the **FILE** tab, and then click **Close** to close the template.

| QUICK REFERENCE | Create a Project Template |

1. Determine and select the scheduling standard of Start or Finish date.
2. Select project scheduling of manual or automatic.
3. Enter in the main headings (summary tasks) and other structure in the WBS that may be common among projects.
4. Click the File tab, and then click Save As.
5. Type a name for the template in the File name box.
6. Click the Save as type arrow, and then click the Project Template option.
7. Click Save, and then click Save again.

Using a Custom Project Template

Once a custom template is created, you can use it to begin a future project plan. The template can also be shared with other members of your organization for project plan consistency. Templates can be stored in locations specified by the creator or a Templates folder that is usually located in the Users\defaults\AppData\Roaming\Microsoft\Templates folder on your computer's hard drive or company network drive.

PM2.21 To Use a Custom Project Template

a. Click the **FILE** tab, and then click **Open**.

> **Troubleshooting**
> If Project 2013 is not open, open Project 2013 and in the left pane click the **Open Other Projects** link.

b. Click **Computer**, and then browse to the location where you store your files. Click the **file type** arrow, and then click **Project Templates**. Click **pm01ws02EventTemplate_LastFirst.mpt** from the available templates list, and then click **Open**.

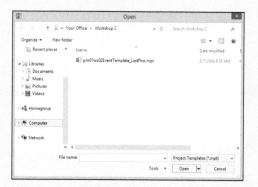

Figure 69   Open dialog box for Project Template search

c. Click **FILE**, and then click **Save As**. Click **Computer**, and then navigate to the location where you store your files. Verify the Save as type is **Project**, and then click **Save** 🖫. A new project named **pm01ws02EventTemplate_LastFirst.mpp** is created.

> **Troubleshooting**
> If the Save as type is Project Template, click the Save as type arrow and select Project.

d. Close the template, and then click **Close** ☒ to close Project.

e. Submit files as directed by your instructor.

1. What is the best Project view for identifying the critical path?

2. What is a Work Breakdown Structure?

3. Define a work resource, material resource, and cost resource.

4. What is the purpose of the Team Planner view?

5. Explain how resource assignments can change task durations.

6. How is elapsed time different than duration?

7. What is the purpose of the Overallocated Resources report?

8. When copying Project 2013 data to paste in other applications, what is the difference between selecting Copy from the Clipboard group of the Task tab and Copy Picture from the Clipboard group of the Task tab?

9. Identify at least two ways of sharing information between Project 2013 and Excel 2013.

10. Why would a project manager use a Project 2013 template to begin a project?

Key Terms

Crashing   68
Effort-driven scheduling   67
Elapsed duration   74
Indenting   57
Leveling   68
Outdenting   57

Overallocated   68
Project summary task   92
Project template   93
Recurring task   76
Resource Sheet view   62
Slack   54

Subtask   57
Summary task   57
Team Planner   73
Tracking   78
Work Breakdown Structure (WBS)   56

Define and display a WBS code (p. 61)

View resource assignments in Team Planner view (p. 73)

Set new project tasks to effort-driven (p. 69)

Create project resources (p. 63)

Identify the critical path (p. 54)

Hide tasks in a WBS (p. 59)

Assign Project resources (p. 65)

Create and assign project resources (p. 62)

Add a Project summary task (p. 92)

Create a WBS (p. 57)

Create a work breakdown structure (p. 56)

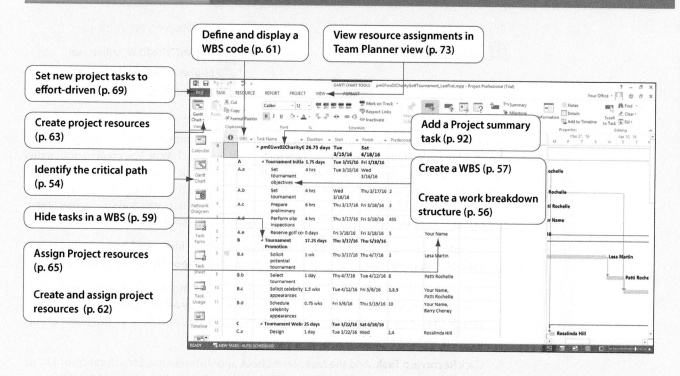

Export Project information into Excel (p. 84)

Begin a Project from a Project template (p. 94)

Create a Project template (p. 96)

Use a custom Project template (p. 97)

Share project information with Microsoft Excel (p. 83)

Use and create Project templates (p. 93)

View reports in Project (p. 79)

Create Project reports (p. 78)

Copy data into an Excel workbook and a Word document (p. 81)

Copy and paste Project information to other applications (p. 80)

Copy and paste a picture of the Calendar view into Word (p. 82)

Import Project information from Excel (p. 86)

Adjust the imported Project tasks from Excel (p. 89)

Change task duration by adding resources (p. 70)

Change task durations by adding resources (p. 67)

Change a duration using the Work form in Split view (p. 72)

Set a task duration to elapsed time (p. 75)

Enhance a project schedule with elapsed duration and recurring tasks (p. 74)

Create a recurring task (p. 77)

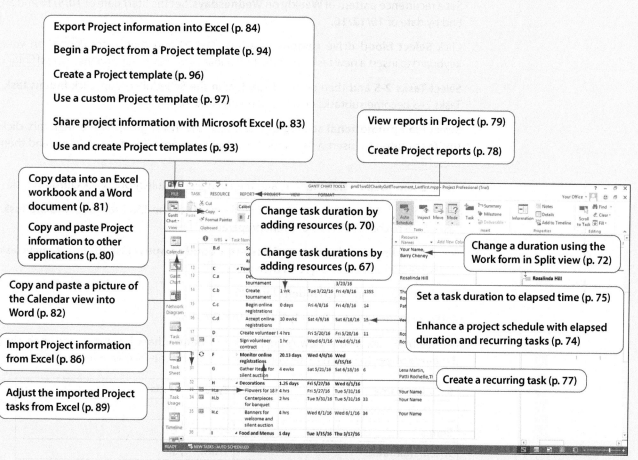

Figure 70 Final Charity Golf Tournament Project

Student data file needed:

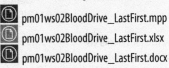 pm01ws02BloodDrive.mpp

You will save your files as:

pm01ws02BloodDrive_LastFirst.mpp

pm01ws02BloodDrive_LastFirst.xlsx

pm01ws02BloodDrive_LastFirst.docx

Organizing a Blood Drive at Your Community College

You continue working with the student senate of your community college by planning a blood drive to promote a cause that saves millions of lives each year. You created your initial task list using Microsoft Project. Now you will create a work breakdown structure, assign your project team members' duties, and work with adjusting the project schedule to fit your project needs. The blood drive will still occur on October 14, 2016; you and your project team are available to work on this project Monday through Wednesday, 8:00 A.M. to 12:00 P.M.

a. Navigate to the location of your student data files and open **pm01ws02 BloodDrive.mpp**. Save the Project file as **pm01ws02BloodDrive_LastFirst.mpp**.

b. You want to be sure you have enough volunteers for the number of appointments set, so you decide to check each week on the appointment list by adding a recurring task. Select **Check site arrangements** (Task 10). Click the **TASK** tab, and then in the Insert group, click the Task list arrow.

c. Click **Recurring Task**. Add the task name Check appointment list. Set a duration of 1 hour. Set a recurrence pattern of **Weekly** on **Wednesdays**. Set the Start date of **10/5/16** and an End by date of **10/12/16**.

d. Click **Select blood drive campus location** (Task 1) and then press ⎡Insert⎤ on your keyboard to insert a new task. Enter the task name Event planning, and then press ⎡Enter⎤.

e. Select **Tasks 2-5** and then on the **TASK** tab, in the Schedule group, click **Indent task**. Tasks 2–5 become subtasks of Event Planning (Task 1).

f. Select **Plan promotional strategies** (Task 6). In the Insert group of the TASK tab, click the **Task** button to insert a new task. Enter the task name Event preparation, and then press ⎡Enter⎤.

g. Select **Event preparation** (Task 6), and then in the Schedule group, click **Outdent** task.

h. Select Tasks 7–18, and then in the Schedule group of the TASK tab, click **Indent Task**. Tasks 7–18 become subtasks of Event preparation (Task 6).

i. Select **Post directional arrows and posters around campus** (Task 19). Insert a new task and name the task Event day, and then press ⎡Enter⎤.

j. **Outdent** Task 19, and then **Indent** Tasks 20–21.

k. Add the summary tasks (Tasks 1, 6, 19) to the **Timeline**.

l. On the TASK tab, in the View group, click the **Gantt Chart** list arrow, and then click **Resource Sheet** to switch to Resource Sheet view. Add the following resources.

Resource Name	Type	Initials
Your Name	Work	YN
Emma Jones	Work	EJ
Joseph Ramirez	Work	JR

m. Click **Gantt Chart** on the View Bar to return to Gantt Chart view. Click the **RESOURCE** tab, and then in the Assignments group, click **Assign Resources**. Assign the resources to the tasks as follows.

Task Name	Resource Names
Event planning	
Select blood drive campus location	Your Name
Set blood drive goal	Your Name
Form a recruitment team	Your Name
Divide team roles and duties	Joseph Ramirez, Your Name
Event preparation	
Plan promotional strategies	Joseph Ramirez
Create promotional materials	Joseph Ramirez
Contact local businesses	Joseph Ramirez
Publicize the blood drive	Joseph Ramirez, Your Name
Schedule appointments	Emma Jones
Check appointment list	**Your Name**
Check site arrangements	Joseph Ramirez
Get visitor parking passes	Your Name
Email visitor parking passes	Your Name
Email appointment reminder messages	Your Name
Event day	
Post directional arrows and posters around campus	Joseph Ramirez

n. Click the **GANTT CHART TOOLS FORMAT** tab, and then click **Project Summary Task.** Change the name of the project summary task (Task 0) to Blood Drive.

o. Right-click the Task Name column, and then click **Insert Column**. Scroll through the list and click **WBS**. Adjust the WBS column width.

p. Click the **PROJECT** tab, and then click **WBS-Define Code**. Define the code with Level 1) **Numbers**; Level 2) **Uppercase Letters**; Level 3) **Lowercase Letters**.

q. Hide the Task Mode column.

r. **Copy** the entire Entry table and paste it into a blank Excel workbook. Adjust the column widths if necessary. **Save** the workbook in the location you store your files as pm01ws02BloodDrive_LastFirst.

s. **Close** Excel.

t. **Copy** the entire Entry table and paste it into a blank Word Document. **Save** the document in the location you store your files as pm01ws02BloodDrive_LastFirst.

u. **Close** Word, and then **close** Project.

v. Save your project, and then submit files as directed by your instructor.

Student data file needed:

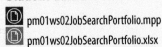 pm01ws02JobSearchPortfolio.mpp
pm01ws02JobSearchPortfolio.xlsx

You will save your file as:

 pm01ws02JobSearchPortfolio_LastFirst.mpp

Planning Your Job Search Portfolio

You have started planning your professional portfolio to use during the interview process since you will be graduating in May 2016 from your program of study at your local college. You have an initial list of tasks already added into a Project file. Now you will add summary tasks, import tasks from Excel, and assign resources to your project to complete your project plan.

a. Navigate to the location of your student data files and open **pm01ws02JobSearch Portfolio.mpp**. Save the Project file as **pm01ws02JobSearchPortfolio_LastFirst.mpp**.

b. Select **Purchase portfolio supplies** (Task 1), and then insert a new task. Name the new task Portfolio Planning. Indent Tasks 2–11 to make them subtasks of Task 1.

c. Select (Task 12). Insert a new task, and then name the task Interview Planning. **Outdent** Task 12.

d. Indent **Tasks 13-16** to make them subtasks of Interview Planning (Task 12).

e. Select **Write resume** (Task 5), and then insert a new task. Name the task Resume.

f. Indent Tasks 6–8 to make them subtasks of Resume (Task 5).

g. Move **Send resumes to potential employers** (Task 14) to the Task 9 position. Note how the task becomes a subtask of Task 5.

> **Troubleshooting**
>
> If Send resumes to potential employers (Task 9) did not become a subtask of Task 5, select the task and indent it.

h. Your project resources are saved in an Excel workbook, so you will **import** the resources. Click the **FILE** tab, and then click **Open**. Click **Computer** and browse to the location of your student data files. Change the file type to **Excel Workbook(*.xlsx)**. Select **pm01ws02JobSearchPortfolio.xlsx** and click **Open**.

i. Click **Next**. Click **New map** and click **Next**. Click **Append the data to the active project** and click **Next**. Click **Resources** under Select the types of data you want to import. Be sure Import includes headers is checked, and then click **Next**. Click the **Source worksheet name** arrow, and then click **Sheet1**. In the Resource Name field, click the arrow on (not mapped) and select **Name**. Click **Finish**.

j. Switch to Resource Sheet view to view the added resources.

k. Return to Gantt Chart view and in a method of your choice, assign the resources as shown.

Task Name	Resource Names
Portfolio Planning	
Purchase portfolio supplies	Your Name
Get an unofficial transcript	Your Name
Identify references	Your Name
Resume	
Write resume	Your Name
Edit resume	James Yang, Your Name
Create a resume in PDF format	Your Name
Send resumes to potential employers	Your Name
Conduct online job search	Your Name
Write a cover letter	Your Name
Gather work examples for portfolio	Your Name
Compile portfolio	Your Name
Interview Planning	
Obtain interview attire	Your Name
Obtain attaché case for interviewing	Your Name
Conduct a mock interview	Career Resource Center

l. The resource assignments have resulted in overallocation. To remove the overallocation, click the **RESOURCE** tab. In the View group, select **Team Planner**.

m. Right-click Your Name and then click **Scroll to Task**. From the Team Planner view, you can see the overallocation is occurring on February 1.

n. Return to **Gantt Chart** view. Double-click Obtain interview attire (Task 15), and then set a **Constraint date** of **4/5/16**.

o. Click **Obtain attaché case for interviewing** (Task 16). If necessary, click the **TASK** tab. In the Properties group, click **Details**.

p. Right-click the Split View, and then click **Work**. Change your work hours of **Obtain attaché case for interviewing** to **0 hours**. Click **OK**. The overallocation has now been corrected.

q. Add **Task 15** as an additional predecessor to **Conduct a mock interview** (Task 17).

r. Right-click the Task Name column, and then click **Insert Column**. Scroll through the list and click **WBS**. Adjust the WBS column width.

s. Click the **PROJECT** tab, and then click **WBS-Define Code**. Define the code with Level 1) **Numbers**; Level 2) **Uppercase Letters**; Level 3) **Lowercase Letters**.

t. Click **Network Diagram** to view the project's critical path. Return to Gantt Chart view.

u. Export the project data to Excel by clicking the **FILE** tab, and then **Save As**. Browse to where you store your files. Enter the File name pm01ws02JobSearchPortfolio_LastFirst, and then in the Save as type, select Excel Workbook. Click **Save**. Click **Next**. Click **Project Excel Template**. Click **Finish**. Click **OK** on the warning dialog box.

v. If necessary, return to your pm01ws02JobSearchPortfolio_LastFirst.mpp project file.

w. On the VIEW tab, in the Data group, filter the project to display Summary Tasks. Select the summary tasks, and then add them to the Timeline.

x. Save your project with the Entry table filtered, and close Project.

y. Submit the project files as directed by your instructor.

Perform 1: Perform in Your Career

Student data file needed:
 pm01ws02BusinessPlan.mpp

You will save your files as:
 pm01ws02BusinessPlan_LastFirst.mpp
pm01ws02BusinessPlan_LastFirst.docx or
pm01ws02BusinessPlan_LastFirst.xlsx

Preparing a Business Plan

You have a start to your new Virtual Assistant business plan in Project. You have decided to add more detail to your plan by creating a work breakdown structure and adding project resources. You also want to share your data with family members who do not have Project 2013 software.

a. Navigate to the location of your student data files and open **pm01ws02BusinessPlan.mpp**. Save the Project file as **pm01ws02BusinessPlan_LastFirst.mpp**.

b. Create a minimum of **two work resources**. Assign resources to each of your subtasks.

c. If necessary, correct any **overallocation** of your resources by changing resource assignments, modifying task relationships, setting task constraints, or modifying work hours.

d. Create a Work Breakdown Structure with a minimum of **three logical summary tasks**.

e. Add a **WBS** column, and then define a WBS code.

f. If necessary, hide the **Task Mode** column.

g. Add the project's summary tasks to the **Timeline**.

h. **Share** your data in a Word document or Excel workbook. As directed by your instructor, explain why you chose Word or Excel and what steps you took to share the project's data.

i. **Save** your project, and then submit files as directed by your instructor.

MODULE CAPSTONE

Student data file needed:

 pm01mp1BathroomRemodel.mpp

You will save your files as:

 pm01mp1BathroomRemodel_LastFirst.mpp

pm01mp1BathroomRemodelTemplate_LastFirst.mpt

Bathroom Remodel Project

The Painted Paradise Resort and Spa takes great pride in its high-quality guest rooms. After management reviewed guest satisfaction survey results, it was determined that 20 bathrooms need updating. To keep the projects on task, you have been asked to create a bathroom remodel template that can be used on all the remodeling projects.

a. Start **Project**, and then open **pm01mp1BathroomRemodel** from the location where you store your files. Save file as **pm01mp1BathroomRemodel_LastFirst**, using your last and first name.

b. Click the **PROJECT** tab, and then in the Properties group, click **Project Information**. Set the project start date to 7/11/16. Click **OK**.

c. In the Properties group, click **Change Working Time**. Adjust the working times to 10:00 A.M.–6:00 P.M. Set Mondays to nonworking time. Set Saturdays to working time.

d. Select Tasks 2–4. In the Schedule group on the **TASK** tab, indent the tasks. This makes Tasks 2–4 subtasks of Task 1.

e. Select Tasks 6–8, and then indent the tasks. This makes Tasks 6–8 subtasks of Task 5.

f. Select Tasks 9–15. On the **TASK** tab, in the Insert group, click **Summary** to create a summary task. Name the summary task Selecting Materials.

g. Select Tasks 2–4. In the Schedule group on the **TASK** tab, click **Link the Selected Tasks** to link the tasks in a Finish-to-Start relationship.

h. Select Tasks 6–8 and create a Finish-to-Start relationship.

i. Create a Start-to-Start relationship between **Tasks 4–6**.

j. Link Tasks 8 and 10.

k. Link the remaining tasks with a Finish-to-Start relationship.

l. Click the **VIEW** tab, and then in the Data group, click the **Filter arrow**. Select **Summary Tasks** to filter for the project's summary tasks.

m. Select the Summary Tasks, and then in the Properties group on the TASK tab, click **Add to Timeline** to add the summary tasks to the Timeline. Remove the filter.

n. Add the note Consider purchasing in bulk. to Task 9, Selecting Materials.

o. Right-click the **Task Mode** column and click **Hide Column** to remove the column from the Entry table.

p. Right-click the **Task Name** column and insert a column. Click **WBS** to add the WBS column to the Entry table. Adjust the width of the WBS column as necessary.

q. On the PROJECT tab, in the Properties group, click **WBS** and then click **Define Code**. Define the WBS code first by **Uppercase Letters**, then by **Lowercase Letters**, and then by **Number**.

r. Click the **FILE** tab, and then click **Print**. Click the **Page Setup** link. Click the **HEADER** tab, and then click **Right**. Add your name to the right-side header.

s. Click the **GANTT CHART TOOLS FORMAT** tab and in the Show/Hide group add a Project Summary Task. Rename the Project Summary Task Bathroom Remodel Template.

t. Since this will be a template, you will not assign resources. Save the project as a template. Name the template pm01mp1BathroomRemodelTemplate_LastFirst.

u. Submit the project files as directed by your instructor.

Problem Solve 1

Student data file needed:

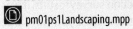 pm01ps1Landscaping.mpp

You will save your files as:

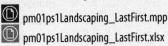 pm01ps1Landscaping_LastFirst.mpp
pm01ps1Landscaping_LastFirst.xlsx

Landscaping Project

You are the manager of the buildings and grounds crew at the Painted Paradise Resort and Spa. You have been assigned to update the landscaping around the resort property. Although you will hire an outside contractor to complete most of the work, you were given an MS Project file to use from a former landscaping job completed at the resort. When you open the file, you notice there are several errors in the project such as overallocation, types of relationships, calendar, length of project, and resource assignments. However, you believe it is easier to correct the MS Project file versus creating a new project.

a. Navigate to the location where you store your files and open **pm01ps1Landscaping.mpp**. Save the file where you store your files as pm01ps1Landscaping_LastFirst using your last and first name.

b. Using the PROJECT tab, set the project start date to **April 4, 2016**.

c. Set all current project tasks to Auto Scheduled by selecting the tasks, and then on the TASK tab, in the Tasks group, click **Auto Schedule**. Set new project tasks to be Auto Scheduled.

d. Due to the heat of the afternoon, the laborers won't work past 1:00 P.M. Adjust your project calendar to the work times of 7:00 A.M.–1:00 P.M. Monday–Friday. Set May 30, 2016 as a calendar exception. Name the exception Memorial Day. Set July 4, 2016 as an additional calendar exception. Name the exception Fourth of July.

e. Switch to Resource Sheet view and replace Your Name with your actual first and last name. You notice resource overallocation on the project plan. One reason there is overallocation is that you are assigned to summary tasks as well as subtasks, which is causing Project to double-schedule you. Remove yourself as a resource from all summary tasks.

f. After removing your name as a resource from the summary tasks, you are still overallocated. Review the project. Note that Task 7, Drawings, has a start date before Task 5, Determine budget. Create an FS relationship between Task 5 and Task 7.

g. Create an FS relationship between Task 6 and Task 12.

h. Create an FS relationship between Task 11 and Task 22.

i. On the TASK tab, in the View group, click the **Gantt Chart** button arrow to switch to Resource Sheet view. Add an additional work resource of **General contractor**. Assign the initials of GC.

j. Add a third resource of **General labor**. Assign the initials of GL. Assign the Max. Units of 300% to give you the availability of assigning three workers to each task. Return to Gantt Chart view.

k. On the VIEW tab, in the Split View group, select Details. Right-click the **details pane** and select **Work**.

l. Select **Task 7, Drawings**. Assign yourself 0 hours of work. Assign General contractor as an additional resource.

m. Repeat Step l for Tasks 8 and 9.

n. Remove yourself as a resource from Tasks 12–20.

o. Assign the General labor to Task 10 to assist with securing the proper permits. Select **Reduce duration but keep the same amount of work**. The duration of Task 10 is now 3.5 days.

p. Select **Task 12**. Assign one **General labor** resource. Select **Task 13**. Assign three **General labor** resources by entering 300% in the Units column of the Work form.

q. Assign three **General labor** resources for Tasks 14–16. Select **Task 17**, and then assign the **General contractor** resource.

r. Select **Task 18**, and then assign three **General labor** resources by entering 300% in the Units column of the Work form.

s. Select **Task 19**, and then assign one **General labor** resource. Select **Task 20**, and then assign three **General labor** resources.

t. Select **Tasks 22–23** and add the **General contractor** as an additional resource. For both tasks, select **Increase the amount of work but keep the same duration** if necessary.

u. Close the split view. Hide the Task Mode Column. Add a **WBS** column, and then adjust the width of the WBS column.

v. Using the **VIEW** tab, filter the Entry table for Summary Tasks. Using the **TASK** tab, add the four summary tasks to the Timeline. Return to the VIEW tab, and remove the filter.

w. On the **GANTT CHART TOOLS FORMAT** tab, add a **Project Summary Task** to your project and rename the task Landscaping 2016.

x. Add your name as a right-side header of the Gantt chart.

y. Export your project data to Excel by selecting the **FILE** tab, click **Save As** and then in a location where you store your files, save the project as an Excel workbook.

z. Submit your project files as directed by your instructor.

Problem Solve 2

Student data file needed:

📄 pm01ps2PlantRelocation.mpt

You will save your file as:

📄 pm01ps2PlantRelocation_LastFirst.mpp

Manufacturing Project

Your company, Falu Fabricating, has grown over the past ten years and the old production shop floor no longer has the proper space size for your current production needs. Your company has acquired another location and you have been put in charge of the team to plan the relocation. An MS Project template has been started for you but it contains overallocated resources. You will fix the overallocated resources to determine the earliest date your company could begin production in the new facility.

a. Navigate to the location where you store your files and open **pm01ps2PlantRelocation. mpt**. Save the file to the location where you store your files as a MS Project file with the name pm01ps2PlantRelocation_LastFirst.

b. Switch to Resource Sheet view and change the resource Your Name to your first and last name. Return to Gantt Chart view.

c. Click the **RESOURCE** tab, and then in the View group, click **Team Planner**. Right-click your name, and then click **Scroll to Task**. View the resource overallocations, and then click **Gantt Chart** on the View Bar.

d. Select **Task 5, Computers and other technology**. Click the **TASK** tab, and then in the Properties group, click **Details** to open the split view. Right-click the form and select **Work**. Assign yourself 0 hours of work for Task 5.

e. Select **Task 6**, and then assign yourself 0 hours of work for Task 6.

f. Change the Predecessor of Task 6 to 5. Change the Predecessor of Task 8 to 6.

g. Select **Task 10**. Change the hours of work for each resource to 40 hours. You notice this decreased the duration of this task to one week. You know the team won't be able to work all 40 hours in one week so you want to extend the finish date of the task. Double-click **Task 10** to open the Task Information dialog box. On the GENERAL tab, change the finish date to 9/21/15.

h. You note there is still overallocation of one of your resources. To correct the overallocation, change the predecessor of Task 13 to include Task 11.

i. Close the split view. Click the **VIEW** tab, in the Split View group, select **Timeline** and then in the Data group, filter for **Summary Tasks**. Select the Summary Tasks, and then click the **TASK** tab. In the Properties group, click **Add to Timeline**.

j. Return to the **VIEW** tab and remove the filter.

k. Hide the Task Mode and Indicators columns.

l. Click the **GANTT CHART TOOLS FORMAT** tab. In the Show/Hide group, select **Outline Number** and **Project Summary Task**. Change the name of the Project Summary Task to Plant Relocation.

m. Click the **VIEW** tab, and then in the Zoom group click **Entire Project** to view all project tasks in the Gantt Chart.

n. Save and close your project plan. Submit the **pm01ps2PlantRelocation_LastFirst** file as directed by your instructor.

Perform 1: Perform in Your Life

Student data file needed:
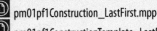 No data file needed

You will save your files as:
pm01pf1Construction_LastFirst.mpp
pm01pf1ConstructionTemplate_LastFirst.mpt

Basement Construction Project

You built a new home two years ago but didn't have the funds to finish the lower level. You believe you have saved enough to complete this project. You will be finishing approximately 8,000 square feet. The lower level already has the electrical and the plumbing in place and has passed inspection. You will plan for the construction of walls, bathroom, cabinetry, flooring, and finishing touches such as painting and trim. Identify your project resources, those who will help you with your project. Determine if you will do the work by yourself or hire outside contractors to assist with some of the work. Determine if you will need to rent any equipment. Decide if you have to consider neighborhood restrictions or any zoning regulations.

a. Start a new Project 2013 file. Save your project as pm01pf1Construction_LastFirst.

b. Select a start date or a finish date. Explain to your instructor why you selected either start or finish date.

c. Select a task scheduling mode of auto scheduled or manually scheduled. Explain to your instructor which mode you selected and why.

d. Set your project tasks to effort-driven.

e. Adjust the project calendar to reflect appropriate working times and days for your project needs.

f. Enter a minimum of 30 task names and task durations.

g. Add a minimum of three milestones.

h. Create a minimum of three summary tasks to develop a Work Breakdown Structure.

i. Add the summary tasks to the timeline.

j. Link your tasks. Give consideration to appropriate task relationships. Not all tasks should have an FS relationship.

k. Create a minimum of three resources, including yourself as one of the resources. Assign resources to the tasks as appropriate. If necessary, use the split view to adjust work hours.

l. Remove any overallocation of resources.

m. View the critical path in the Network Diagram. Add your name to the header of the Network Diagram.

n. Add your name to the header of the Gantt Chart view.

o. Hide the Task Mode column. Add the WBS column. Define the WBS code.

p. Add a task note to at least one task.

q. Add a project summary task.

r. Save your project.

s. Save your project as a template. Name the template pm01pf1ConstructionTemplate_LastFirst.

t. Submit your files as directed by your instructor.

Perform 2: Perform in Your Career

Student data file needed:

 pm01pf2ConventionPlan.xlsx

You will save your file as:

 pm01pf2ConventionPlan_LastFirst.mpp

Convention Planning Project

The organization you work for sells and services life-saving devices for water safety. Next summer, your organization is hosting a 1-day convention to promote new and improved life-saving devices in your industry. You have been asked to plan this convention. Because you know planning a convention involves many steps, and many resources will be involved, you decide to use MS Project 2013 to plan the event. You had entered your list of tasks in Excel 2013; so, to save time, you will import these tasks into MS Project. Because you have not yet set a date for the convention, but know it must be in the summer of 2017, you will schedule your project by Start Date and use MS Project to help you predict when the event should be scheduled. Because there are many tasks and task relationships, you will set your project to Auto Schedule.

a. Open a blank project file, and then save the project as pm01pf2ConventionPlan_LastFirst.mpp in a location where you store your files.

b. Set the start date of the project to **August 1, 2016**.

c. Set the project's new tasks to **Auto Schedule**.

d. Set new tasks to **effort-driven**.

e. Display the View Bar and the Timeline if necessary.

f. Adjust the project calendar to make Fridays from 1:00 P.M.–5:00 P.M. nonworking time. Add an exception of your choice.

g. Browse to the location of your student data files and **import** the tasks from the **pm01pf2ConventionPlan.xlsx** workbook.

h. Adjust column widths as necessary. Wrap text as necessary. Hide the Task Mode column and add the WBS column. Define the WBS code.

i. Select **Tasks 1–13** and add a summary task. Name the summary task Convention Initiation.

j. Select **Tasks 15–43** and insert a summary task. Name the summary task Convention Planning.

k. Select **Tasks 45-48** and indent the tasks to make them subtasks.

l. Select **Task 50, Evaluations**, and then insert a blank task. Name the new blank task Convention Close Out. Demote Tasks 51–57 to make them subtasks of Convention Close Out, Task 50.

m. After reviewing the tasks, assign logical task relationships. Consider relationships such as Start-to-Start, Finish-to-Finish, or Finish-to-Start.

n. Add your name as a resource. Create a list of a minimum of four more resources to help you with the planning of this event.

o. Assign resources to tasks as you see appropriate. Give consideration to tasks having more than one resource assignment.

p. Adjust resources assignment or work hours to remove any overallocation that may have occurred during resource assignments.

q. Add a Project Summary Task and give the Project Summary Task a descriptive name.

r. Add the project's summary tasks to the project's Timeline.

s. Add your first and last name to the right-side header of the Gantt Chart, Network Diagram, and Calendar views.

t. Review your project, and then save and close your project. Submit the project file as directed by your instructor.

24 Hours calendar   a calendar that assigns a schedule with continuous work such as a project that must work around the clock.

A

Auto Scheduled   a scheduling option where the project schedule is calculated based on the project's calendar, project tasks and task durations, task dependencies, resource assignments, and any constraint dates assigned to tasks.

B

Backstage view   location where you manage your project file and perform tasks such as saving, printing, and setting project options.

Baseline   is a record of each task at a point in time from which you will track project progress.

C

Calendar view   a view that displays tasks as bars on a calendar in a monthly format.

Constraint   is a limitation set on a task.

Cost resource   independent cost you want to associate with a task.

Crashing   adding more work resources to a project to get the project tasks done faster and shorten the project's duration.

Critical path   tasks (or a single task) that determine the project's Finish date (or Start date).

Critical task   a task that must be completed on time in order to meet the project's Finish date (or Start date).

Current date   today's date as determined by your computer's clock.

E

Effort-driven scheduling   the default method of scheduling in Project in which the duration of a task is shortened as resources are added or lengthened as resources are removed from a task.

Elapsed duration   ignores any project or resources working and nonworking times and schedules the task(s) to 24 hours a day.

Entry table   location in which to enter task information; located to the left of the Gantt chart and which contains columns and rows similar to Microsoft Excel 2013.

F

Finish date   the date Project will use to begin scheduling tasks to calculate the Start date.

G

Gantt chart   the graphical representation of the tasks listed in the Entry table; tasks are shown against a timeline displayed as horizontal bars in which the length of the bar is determined by the activities durations and start/finish dates.

Gantt Chart view   a view that displays tasks, task durations, and task dependencies in a Gantt chart with horizontal bars and is the default view in Project.

I

Indenting   moves a task to the right in the Entry table and makes it a lower level task in a Work Breakdown Structure.

Indicators column   a column in the Entry table view that will display an icon that provides further information about a task such as task constraint, task calendar, or task note.

L

Lag time   moves a successor task forward in time so the Start dates between the tasks are further apart.

Lead time   moves a successor task back in time so the two tasks overlap and the Start date between the tasks gets closer.

Leveling   a process of correcting overallocated resources to ensure no resource is assigned more hours than available work hours.

M

Manually Scheduled   a scheduling option where task dates are not calculated or adjusted by Project's scheduling engine, even if changes to related tasks are made.

Material resource   a resource consumed during the project.

Milestone   a task that is used to communicate project progress or mark a significant point in a project.

N

Network Diagram view   displays tasks in a detailed box along with clearly representing task dependencies with link lines and displays critical path.

Night Shift calendar   assigns a schedule that is sometimes referred to as the "graveyard" shift schedule of Monday night through Saturday morning, 11:00 P.M. to 8:00 A.M. with an hour off for break.

Nonworking day   a day which Project will not schedule work to occur.

Note   acts as a sticky note for a task providing further information or instructions regarding a task.

O

Outdenting   moves a task to the left in the Entry table and makes it a higher level in a Work Breakdown Structure.

Overallocated   when a resource is assigned to more work than available working hours.

P

Predecessor task   a task that must be completed before the next task can start.

Project goal   the desired result of a project upon completion.

Project Information dialog box   the dialog box used to update various aspects of a project such as the project's start date, status date, current date, and project base calendar.

Project management   a process of initiating, planning, executing, monitoring, and closing a project's tasks and resources in order to accomplish a project's goal.

Project manager the person responsible for overseeing all the details of the project plan.

Project summary task summarizes the timeline of your project and displays the total duration of your project.

Project template a Project file that contains sample project information such as tasks, durations, resources, and other project data.

Q

Quick Access Toolbar a series of small icons for commonly used commands.

R

Recurring task a task that repeats at regular intervals.

Resource Sheet view a view commonly used to create resources and present resource information.

Resource work, material, or cost associated with a project task.

Row selector the box containing the row number of a task in the Entry table.

S

Scope what must be completed to deliver a specific product or service.

Select All a button that selects all task and task information in the Entry table.

Slack the time a task can be delayed from its scheduled start date without delaying the project.

Split bar separates the Entry table and the Gantt chart.

Standard calendar Project's default base calendar of 40 hours a week 8:00 A.M. to 12:00 P.M. and 1:00 P.M. to 5:00 P.M.

Start date the date Project will use to begin scheduling tasks to calculate the Finish date.

Status date the date you set to run reports on a project's progress.

Subtask a related task that further defines the summary task.

Successor task a task that has a predecessor.

Summary task a task listed in bold in the Entry table associated with a group of tasks that logically belong together.

T

Task an activity that is completed to reach a project goal.

Task dependency a relationship between tasks that define which task(s) have to finish before the next task(s) can start.

Task duration prediction of time it will take to complete a task.

Task Information the dialog box that includes all the details for a single task.

Task Mode column a column in the Entry table that indicates the mode in which Project will schedule tasks, either manually or automatically.

Task Name column a column in the Entry table where the name of each task is entered.

Team Planner a Project view that shows a project's resources and tasks assigned to each resource.

Timeline a visual representation of the project from start to finish.

Timescale displays the unit of measure that determines the length of the Gantt bars in the Gantt chart.

Tracking recording the actual progress of the project's tasks.

V

View Bar a vertical bar on the left-hand side of the Project window that contains buttons for quick access to different Project views.

W

Work Breakdown Structure (WBS) a method of organizing tasks in a hierarchical structure.

Work resource people and equipment associated with a project task.

Index